History of Fluvial Hydraulics

R.J. GARDE

Professor Emeritus
Civil Engineering Department
University of Roorkee
Roorkee, (Uttarakhand)

PUBLISHING FOR ONE WORLD

NEW AGE INTERNATIONAL (P) LIMITED, PUBLISHERS

New Delhi • Bangalore • Chennai • Cochin • Guwahati • Hyderabad
Jalandhar • Kolkata • Lucknow • Mumbai • Ranchi
Visit us at **www.newagepublishers.com**

Published by New Age International (P) Ltd., Publishers
First Edition: 1995
Reprint: 2009

Branches:

- 36, Malikarjuna Temple Street, Opp. ICWA, Basavanagudi, **Bangalore**. ✆ (080) 26677815
- 26, Damodaran Street, T. Nagar, **Chennai**. ✆ (044) 24353401
- CE-39/1016, Carrier Station Road, Near Paulson Park Hotel, Ernakulam South,**Cochin.** ✆ (0484) 4051303
- Hemsen Complex, Mohd. Shah Road, Paltan Bazar, Near Starline Hotel, **Guwahati**. ✆ (0361) 2543669
- No. 105, 1st Floor, Madhiray Kaveri Tower, 3-2-19, Azam Jahi Road, Nimboliadda, **Hyderabad**. ✆ (040) 24652456
- RDB Chambers (Formerly Lotus Cinema) 106A,1st Floor, S.N. Banerjee Road, **Kolkata**. ✆ (033) 22275247
- 16-A, Jopling Road, **Lucknow**. ✆ (0522) 2209578
- 142C, Victor House, Ground Floor, N.M. Joshi Marg, Lower Parel, **Mumbai**. ✆ (022) 24927869
- 22, Golden House, Daryaganj, **New Delhi**. ✆ (011) 23262370, 23262368

ISBN: 978-81-224-0815-7

Rs. 395.00

C-09-06-3720

Printed in India at Glorious Printers, Delhi.
Typeset at Jayanti Graphics Pvt. Ltd., New Delhi.

PUBLISHING FOR ONE WORLD
NEW AGE INTERNATIONAL (P) LIMITED, PUBLISHERS
4835/24, Ansari Road, Daryaganj, New Delhi-110002
Visit us at **www.newagepublishers.com**

Preface

THE STUDY OF HISTORY of any subject provides an opportunity to know about the earlier civilizations, about the problems they faced, and about the manner in which those were managed. Such a study also throws light on how the scientific thought, methods of analysis, and experimentation developed with the passage of time. Finally, it gives to the men of the past and present who have contributed to the development of the subject, their just due and it also provides to those of the present with the guide for orientation of their own endeavours. Such an integrated appreciation of the historical development of the subject brings a sense of purpose and maturity of thought in the scientific community, which is reflected in their approach to research and its applications. Hence, there is enough justification in the study of the History of Fluvial Hydraulics. Fluvial Hydraulics deals with the hydraulics of the rivers flowing through loose non-cohesive material and transporting the sediment with them.

With this purpose in mind, and more as a continuous process of learning, this study of the History of Fluvial Hydraulics was undertaken. Some difficulties were encountered during the preparation of the manuscript. The first and the foremost was the non-availability of literature and photographs of the scientists and engineers from some of the non English-speaking countries such as Russia. Secondly, certain aspects of Fluvial Hydraulics such as soil erosion, drainage patterns, and sedimentation have been studied in detail by the soil scientists, geologists, and geomorphologists. It was found rather difficult to do full justice to their contributions partly because of the limitation of space and partly because of the limited exposure of the author to their works. Lastly, the author realises that the present study may not have done full justice to the contributions of some of the scientists, and may have inadvertently failed to mention the contribution of a few others. However, his only hope is that this study will stimulate others to collect additional information which can form the basis for a detailed record of the History of Fluvial Hydraulics.

The University Grants Commission (India) provided the U.G.C. Emeritus Fellowship to the author to undertake this work. The author gratefully acknowledges this assistance as well as the permission given by U.G.C. to publish the manuscript in the book form. The author is, in particular, thankful to late Prof. G. Ram Reddy, Chairman, and Prof. S.K. Khanna, former Vice-Chairman of U.G.C. The author is also thankful to Dr. Z.S. Tarapore and Dr. P.P. Vaidyaraman, former directors of the Central Water and Power Research Station, Pune (India), for permitting the author to work at Central Water and Power Research Station.

Several individuals have provided valuable information during the preparation of the manuscript. These include late Professors V.G. Garde and T. Blench, late Brig. R.A. Bagnold, Mr. G.G. Joshi, Mrs. Wei-Yao Kung (Mrs. Ning Chien), and Professors Yuichi Iwagaki, J.L. Bogardi, V.A. Vanoni, D.B. Simons, Bingnan Lin, T. Hayashi, J.R.L. Allen, M.L. Albertson, S.C. Jain, W.H. Graf and J.A. Maza Alvarez. In addition Mrs. Margaret E. Counce, Information Specialist, U.S.D.A., Reston (USA), provided biographical information on G.K. Gilbert, Mrs. M. Siddiqi of the British Council, New Delhi provided biographical sketches of C.M. White, late Sir C.C. Inglis and late Sir G. Lacey, and Mrs. Marlene Janssen of the University of Iowa (USA) provided information on A. Shields and A.A. Kalinske. Mrs. Ujwala Khare helped in translating some material from the German language. The author is indebted to all of them for their assistance. The author is also thankful to Prof. W.H. Graf for according permission to quote some lines from his book on Hydraulics of Sediment Transport, which are translation of portion from Du Buat's treatise.

Pune
August 1995

R.J. GARDE
INSA Senior Scientist
Central Water & Power Research Station
Khadakwasla, Pune

List of Symbols

A	Cross-sectional areas, constant
B	Channel width
b	Pier width
C	Chezy's coefficient
c	Sediment concentration at distance y above the bed
D	Depth of flow
D_{SC}	Maximum scour depth in clear water flow, measured below water surface
D_{SE}	Equilibrium scour depth in sediment transporting flow, measured below water surface
d	Median sediment size, sediment diameter arithmetic mean size of sediment
Fr	Froude number
f	Darcy-Weisbach friction factor
f_1	Lacey's silt factor
K_S	Equivalent sand grain roughness
n	Manning's roughness coefficient
P	Perimeter
Q	Discharge
Q_B, Q_S, Q_T	Bed-load, suspended load, total-load discharge
q	Discharge per unit width of channel
q_B, q_S, q_T	Bed-load, suspended load and total load discharge per unit width of channel
R	Hydraulic radius; bend radius
Re	Reynolds number
S	Channel slope

U	Average velocity of flow in the vertical or section
U_{cr}	Critical average velocity
U_w	Velocity of ripples and dunes
u	Velocity in x direction at a distance y above the bed
u_b	Bottom velocity
u_s	Surface or maximum velocity
u_*	$(= \sqrt{\tau_0/\rho_f})$
v	Velocity in y direction
W	Average width of flow or channel
W'	Submerged weight of particle
w	Velocity in z direction
Z	Exponent of suspended sediment distribution equation

Greek Notations

γ_f	Sepecific weight of fluid
γ_f	Specific weight of sediment
$\Delta\gamma_s$	Difference in the specific weights of sediment and fluid
κ	Karman constant (Kappa)
ε_m	Momentum transfer coefficient
ε_s	Sediment transfer coefficient
μ	Dynamic viscosity of fluid
ν	Kinematic viscosity of fluid
ρ_f	Mass density of fluid
ρ_s	Mass density of sediment
τ_{0c}	Critical shear stress
τ_0	Average shear stress on the bed
ϕ	Angle of repose, Dimensionless transport parameter
ω_0	Fall velocity of a particle under ideal condition

Subscripts and superscripts

b	With respect to bed
c or cr	Pertaining to critical condition
f	Pertaining to fluid
s	Pertaining to sediment
$'$	With respect to grain roughness
$''$	With respect to form roughness

Contents

Chapter 1

Introduction

For engineers and scientists working in any specialisation, it is very instructive and hence desirable to study the historical developments in that and related specialisations. Such an effort provides an opportunity to know about earlier civilisations, the problems they faced and the manner in which they handled the complex situations. It also affords an opportunity to study how the scientific thought and the methods of analysis developed with the passage of time. Lastly, it provides a chance to study the lives of scientists and engineers who made these developments possible and get inspiration from their lives. It is strongly felt that such an integrated appreciation of historical development brings a sense of purpose and maturity to the scientific community which is reflected in their approach to research and in their efforts to solve complex problems of the present. With this purpose in mind and because such a study of History of Fluvial Hydraulics has never been undertaken earlier, the author has been collecting information during the past few years and organising the same. The present work is an outcome of this effort.

Several difficulties are faced in this type of study. First and the foremost is the non-availability of literature from different countries. The second is the language difficulty, and the third is the political barriers which existed till the recent past and which prevented flow of information from one country to other. Fortunately such barriers are fast crumbling and it is hoped that in future more and more information, which was not available earlier, will be available from Russia, China and other countries.

The geologists, geomorphologists and soil scientists have contributed significantly to our overall understanding of the fluvial processes and erosion. The concept of geomorphic cycle which explains the diastrophism through which land mass comes up and then gets gradually eroded through action of rain is very useful.

Different stages of evolution of land surfaces and channels viz. youthful, mature and old also form the basis of geomorphic study. The study of drainage patterns, ordering of streams, study of history of river from the analysis of sediment deposits and effect of changes in climatic conditions (over centuries) on the hydrology and channel charactersitics also form an important aspect of Geomorphology and Fluvial Hydraulics. Another aspect of significance is the mechanics of soil erosion and deposition from small and large areas. All these aspects would directly or indirectly affect the alluvial channel formation and its hydraulics. However, inclusion of survey of progress of thought in these subdisciplines would greatly extend the scope of this work and make it less coherent. Hence, the writer has refrained from the temptation of including details of development in these areas.

The development of Fluvial Hydraulics has been greatly benefited by the contributions of experimental hydraulicians and hydrodynamists of 18th, 19th and the 20th century e.g. Bernoulli, Euler, Lagrange, Navier, Stokes, Chezy, Bazin, Weisbach, Froude, Reynolds, Prandtl and others. However, their contributions have been discussed in an excellent manner by Rouse and Ince (239) in their book on History of Hydraulics. Hence, only those contributions which are of relevance to this study have been briefly discussed here.

A word about the organisation of the material in the book will be in order. A major portion of our knowledge in Fluvial Hydraulics has been gained during the past two centuries. It will not be wrong to say that quantitative Fluvial Hydraulics really started with the development of first bed-load equation by du Boys in 1879. Further, much more progress has been made in the 20th century. Keeping these facts in mind the contributions have been discussed under the following periods:

- Developments up to 1600 A.D.
- Developments during 1600 — 1800 A.D.
- Developments during 1800 — 1900 A.D.
- Developments during 1900 — 1925 A.D.
- Developments during 1925 — 1950 A.D.
- Developments during 1950— 1975 A.D.
- Developments after 1975.

Further, while discussing developments in each period, different ways have been adopted to suit the convenience of presentation. Thus developments up to 1600 A.D. are discussed country-wise; however, contributions during 19th century are discussed topic-wise.

Lastly, it is again stated that because of the constraints of non-availability of material and language barrier, the present study should be considered as the beginning. It is hoped that this study will stimulate engineers from other countries in collecting additional information which can be woven into a more detailed record of the History of Fluvial Hydraulics.

Chapter 2

Developments up to 16th Century

Fluvial Hydraulics is the hydraulics of rivers flowing through loose noncohesive material. Study of literature indicates that not much was known about the Fluvial Hydraulics as a discipline up to 16th century. However, people in different countries had built irrigation canals taking off from alluvial streams, they had built head works, the people faced problems due to sedimentation of canals and floods, and developed some methods of controlling floods and training of the rivers. These general developments that took place in India, China, Mesopotamia (Iraq), Egypt, Greece and Italy during the above mentioned period are briefly discussed below.

DEVELOPMENTS IN INDIA

The developments about irrigation, rivers, and dams in India in the ancient times can be inferred from religious scriptures such as Vedas, Upvedas, Upnishadas, Puranas and Samhitas and from the archaelogical investigations and the tablets found therein. The sage Bhrigu has written two volumes of Samhitas, namely Shilpa-Samhita (Engineering Science) and Jyotisha Samhita (Science of Astrology). In shilpa-samhita Bhrigu deals with: (i) Krishi shastra (agriculture), (ii) Jala-shastra (hydraulics), (iii) Khanti-shastra (metallurgy), (iv) Nauka-shastra (ship building), (v) Rath-shastra (Vehicles), (vi) Agniyan-shastra (rockets), (vii) Vastu-shastra (materials), (viii) Prakar-shastra, (ix) Nagar Rachana-shastra (town planning), and (x) Yantra-shastra (mechanical engineering).

In Jal-shastra the following three characteristics of static water have been mentioned (102) by Bhrigu.

i) the surface of water at rest is level;

ii) the water exerts uniform pressure in all directions;

iii) the pressure of water is equal to its weight, and greater the depth, greater is the pressure.

Nineteen characteristics of flowing water have been mentioned by sage Vashistha (102, 279, 280). Some of these are:

i) The water surface slopes in the direction of flow, and greater the slope, faster is the movement;

ii) In a channel the velocity is largest near the centre and it is reduced near the banks;

iii) The flowing water in a river cross-section is never horizontal; it is higher on one side and lower on the other side;

iv) If flowing water is obstructed, it stops; but it exerts pressure on the obstruction which is proportional to the velocity;

v) Flowing water has an ability to carry gravel, sand, silt and clay. This ability decreases as the velocity of flow is decreased. Hence, for sedimentation the flow velocity should be reduced and for scour it should be increased.

It may be mentioned that there are also some statements about flowing water which are either incomplete or incorrect. Thus, it is mentioned that

Water pressure increases as one goes deeper below the water surface and therefore there it is thicker and heavier than that at the surface.

In this samhita there is also information on dams, how they should be constructed, on water tanks, and wells. There is also discussion about organisation of engineering works. From the Indian literature one can draw the inference that in vedic and postvedic times people seemed to be aware of erosion caused by rivers, control of erosion, embankments, flow diversion, etc. However, all this information is given in spiritual language. More information and additional references on the subject can be found in references (102, 149, 279, 280).

DEVELOPMENTS IN CHINA

From the point of view of sediment, China has some of the most troublesome rivers such as the Yellow river which carries water with a very high sediment concentration. Hence, it is not surprising that from the earlier times Chinese engineers have dealt with sediment transporting rivers and have contributed significantly to our knowledge of Fluvial Hydraulics.

One of the Chinese emperors, Yau, had ordered the regulation of the Chinese rivers; however the man in charge, after building for twelve years was unable to provide the expected protection and fell into disgrace. His son, Yu, continued the efforts and succeeded after eight years to bring the Hwang Ho, the Yangtze Kiang and its tributaries under control. In recognition of these efforts, he was made the emperor. Yu was and is still honoured by construction of Pagodas at various water courses. One plaque attached to the cliff of the Hwang Ho marks the occasion of the construction of a flood way in 2278 B.C. Yu claimed that he was the one who

Great Yu standing on Camel Hill on the banks of the Yellow river.

guided the nine rivers towards sea. According to Yu, river regulation was such that each river was treated according to its characteristics. He was able to control excess sediment from entering into main channel. However, ditches which got filled with sediment were periodically emptied by farmers and they used this fine sediment on their farms (111). Artist's conception of 150 ton, 10 m high statue of Great Yu standing on the Camel Hill on the banks of the Yellow river is shown in the adjoining sketch (115).

Flow diversion as a flood control measure was adopted by the Chinese (131). Marco Polo who visited China in 13th century reported that, "Beyond the city (Hangchau) and enclosing it on that side, there is a ditch about 40 miles in length, very wide and full of water that comes from the river before mentioned. This was excavated by the ancient kings of the province, so that when the river should overflow its banks, the superfluous water might be diverted into this channel."

In some parts of China, old irrigation projects constructed several centuries ago exist and some are still in operating condition. One such project in Chengdu plain in the west of Sichuan basin, was built on the Minjiang river (290). A diversion structure was built on the river by Li Bing, the governor of the Shu region in 316 B.C. The diversion embankment was like a "fish mouth". A canal was dug and just upstream a "sediment and flow excluding weir" was built. The canal was used for irrigation as well as navigation. As mentioned by Xu Muju (290) the structure had been functioning till 1949. Since then some modifications and renovations have been done. Rules for river regulation proposed and as used by Li Bing have been found engraved on the wall of the temple. These rules indicate a very good understanding of the river behaviour by Li Bing. Another astonishing mark of achievements in hydraulic engineering is the complicated net of an irrigation system designed by Chengkuo about 240 B.C. Some of the irrigation canals from that century and the rules for their operation are still in use (111).

C.H. Pan a high officer and river engineer in Ming Dynasty (1368 - 1643 A.D.) devoted himself to studying the problems of the Yellow River for 26 years (1566 - 1591 A.D.). During the later years of his life he wrote a 14-volume treatise on "General Features of River Control" which was published in 1590 and reprinted by the Chinese Hydraulic Engineering Society (197) in 1936. Pan urged that the proper way "to remove the silt deposited on the bed (of the river) was to concentrate the flow (of water) and to maintain the stream by its own current." He noted that the Yellow River was the muddiest one in China and added that "the silt will be deposited unless we have very swift current. In case the flow is divided, the power is reduced, silt will be deposited and finally the river will be silted up."

Pan did not favour dredging as a means of regulating the river, stating that "the depth of the river is from 30 ft (9.14 m) to 70 ft (21.34 m) and its width is from 2000 ft to one mile (0.6 km to 1.6 km). It is saturated with billions of tons of silt. Suppose five miles of river are to be dredged, how many labourers will be employed and how many months and days will be spent on it? And where shall we put this large amount of silt dredged?... To wash out the silt by current is as easy as to melt snow with boiling water. Dredging is used only for small canals and not for the Yellow river."

DEVELOPMENT IN MESOPOTAMIA

Earliest evidence of existence of man in Mesopotamia is that obtained by Solecki in 1951 when he found at Shanidar (north east of Baghdad) four human skeletons appproximately 60,000 years old (i.e. of stone age). At Jarmo, carbonised wheat and barley grains, bones of sheep, cattle, pigs and dogs have been found which indicate intense agricultural activity about 7000 years B.C. (96). This indicates that irrigation was practised at that time.

An early king of Lagash, in Southern Mesopotamia, called Ur-Nina who reigned about 2900 B.C. built a canal called Edin. During 1900 - 1800 B.C. in and around Larsa (Southern Mesopotamia) a bureau of irrigation existed, the head of which had the authority from the king to undertake investigation of new irrigation projects, appointing work force as large as 1800 labourers and authorising opening of sluices. The evidence indicates that the following types of works were undertaken:
(i) excavation of canals, feeder channels and ditches to carry water to farms; (ii) removing silt from irrigation channels; (iii) surveying and fixing the boundaries of fields and reclaiming lands. It is also inferred that the people at that time were conversant with computations related to digging, dredging of canals, etc. Records in this period refer to many canals by name e.g. Hiritum canal, Nubitar canal, Isin canal, Etellum canal, etc. Thus direct and indirect evidence indicates that when Abisare and Samuel ruled Larsa, there was widespread network of irrigation canals, massive deployment of workers for the construction and maintenance of irrigation system, large scale managerial machinery and centralised authority. Canals were also used as waterways for transport. This activity in Southern Mesopotamia decreased around 1700 B.C. and shifted to Central part of Mesopotamia probably due to salinization. Canals were also diverted to weaken the existence of neighbouring states.

In Central and Northern Mesopotamia, similar developments took place. During 4000 - 2300 B.C. very rudimentary irrigation system, viz., flood irrigation system was used for which no complicated control works were required. During 2100 - 1800 B.C. many settlements in the Diyala river (a tributary of the Tigris) basin were abandoned and not recovered for next 400 years. Two possible explanations for this abandonment are probable salinization due to over irrigation and changes in stream course. As pointed out by Jacobson and Adams (146), the semi-arid climate and generally low permeability of soils in Mesopotamia expose the soils to dangerous accumulation of salts and sodium ions which make the soil saline.

In the earlier periods, Mesopotamia was divided in several small states governed by the kings. The sixth king of Babylon, Hammurabi (1711-1669 B.C.)

was able to unify the country for the first time by subjugating these states. He is also credited with unifying the various laws existing in different states at that time and giving what is known as Hammurabi's code. This code contains five laws about irrigation. During 1800 - 625 B.C. there was substantial disruption in settled life in Diyala basin due to conquests by Hammurabi, and Cassites who were Indo-Europeans migrating towards west from Iran.

Irrigation activity flourished in the vicinity of Ninevah (present name Mosul) under the Assyrian king Sennacherib who ruled from 705 - 685 B.C, He built 80 km long paved channel from the Gomel stream to Ninevah, on which an aqueduct was built. This aqueduct, known as Sennacherib's aqueduct, is the oldest in the world of which the remains have survived.

This aqueduct at Jerwan was 22 m wide and it is estimated that it carried a discharge of about 40 m^3/s - 80 m^3/s at full depth. It is also estimated that more than two million stones of size 0.50 m × 0.50 m × 0.50 m were used in its construction. Near Ninevah the canal discharged into a stream called Khosar and water was stored there by building a small dam.

During 626 B.C. - 636 A.D. irrigation activity flourished in the Diyala basin. More and more canals and branch channels were constructed. Link canal between the rivers Tigris and Diyala was constructed to divert water from the Tigris to Diyala and then to farms. This canal known as Katul-Al-Kisrawi had a capacity of about 100 m^3/s - 300 m^3/s, and was 130 km long. Remains of Al-Qantara weir

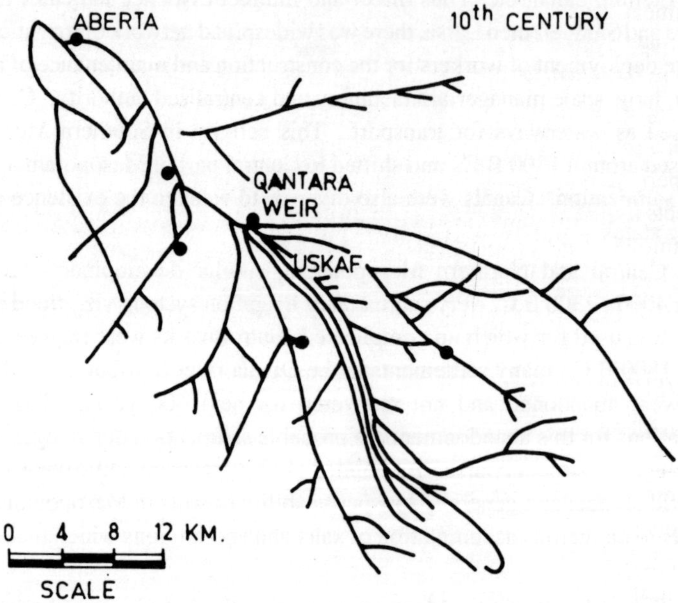

Al-Quantara weir on Naharwan canal

on the Nahrwan canal and head-regulator, and the traces of canals, bridges, etc. on the canals can still be seen. In order to indicate probable competence in understanding the engineering skills, it may be mentioned that all the five branch channels from the Nahrwan canal upstream of Al-Qantara weir were taking off from the outer bank of a sharp bend. This is in conformity with the present day practice which ensures minimum amount of sediment entering the branch.

During the Islamic period (633 - 1258 A.D.) the irrigation activity in Diyala area decreased considerably. This was partly due to silting of canals and nearby areas, and partly due to interference with the irrigation by Mongols. One of their kings, Hulagu, methodically destroyed dikes, headworks and the canals. That destruction impaired the hydraulic activities which never picked up till the 20th century.

It is estimated that the Tigris-Euphrates delta is building up at a rate of about 2 to 2.5 km per hundred years. The ancient city of Ur which was founded about 4000 B.C. on the marshy limit of gulf and which served as the sea port at historic times is now 150 km inside.

Evidence indicates that there have occurred secondary changes in the course of the Tigris. Here, lateral movement of the meander loop is accompanied by very little downward movement of the meanders. Over a period of 4000 years or so the Tigris and the Euphrates have moved laterally less than 30 km.

At high discharges the Tigris and the Euphrates carry high sediment loads; the concentration can be more than 10 000 ppm (119). During the flood, part of the sediment gets deposited on the flood plain and some in the canals. The material removed from the canals is dumped on spoil banks which is carried by wind and rain to the surrounding area. As a result the general level of Mesopotamian plain is rising at the rate of 20 cm every hundred years. As discussed earlier, silting has been a problem with Mesopotamian canals since long. They had to be maintained properly every year by removing silt. An interesting reference to silting and its effects is quoted below. The King Nebuchandnezzar (1146 -1125 B.C.) cursed his enemies thus (96):

> "That Raman that the God of Sources and Rivers fill thy canal with sand and leave thee a prey to famine".

DEVELOPMENTS IN EGYPT

As in Mesopotamia, extensive irrigation systems existed in Egypt around 4000 B.C. There is evidence (239) to indicate that one of the early kings, Menes, first of the Pharaohs, built a masonry dam across the Nile at Memphis about 3000 B.C. King Amenemhet III (1841-1801 B.C.) completed a huge water resources project. Water from the Nile, stored upstream of the dam during floods, was carried through the canal of Joseph to the prehistoric lake Moeris. This was then returned to the Nile during the lean season thereby ensuring water for year round irrigation. This also worked as a flood control method using flow diversion. Around 2500 B.C., a fresh water canal had already been constructed from Cairo to Suez. Between 1900 B.C. and 500 B.C. attempts were made to complete a navigation canal between Mediterranean and Red sea following more or less the same route as the present Suez canal.

Since majority of the above mentioned works were in alluvium, it is inferred that problems of flooding, erosion and silting of channels were encountered by the Egyptians and methods to cope with them were known. There is no significant direct information available about contribution in the field of Fluvial Hydraulics from Egypt.

GREEK AND ITALIAN CONTRIBUTIONS

The civilizations of the Yellow, Indus, Tigris and Euphrates, and Nile which preceded the Greek Civilisation had an influence on the scientific developments in Greece because it is believed that people from these areas moved from one region to other. However, Greek civilisation contributed marginally to the development of Fluvial Hydraulics or river hydraulics. Work attributed to Hippocrates (400 B.C.) clearly implied understanding of differential velocities of settling of different sediment particles; even an apparatus that could be used to demonstrate this principle was described (168). Greeks also used the principle of decantation for the purification of earth as may be learned from Theophratus (168). The contributions of Archimedes (288 - 212 B.C.) in the area of hydrostatics and flotation, tubular screw for pumping water and the screw propeller for ships are well known. Similarly, Hero (150 - 100 B.C.) contributed to our understanding of suction and siphon action and it also seems he understood the continuity equation $Q = AU$, (10). As indicated by Graf (111), far more interesting in our context is that a Greek by the name of Ctesias is said to have written around 250 B.C. a treatise on rivers, the oldest known written contribution to river hydraulics.

Romans were very practical minded and hence instead of carrying scientific progress very far, they excelled in certain engineering achievements, such as sewer and water supply system, aqueducts, etc. Around 1000 B.C. irrigation was practised in Italy. However, in the art of water supply their contribution is very significant. Marcus Vitruvius Pollio (1st century B.C.) wrote 10-volume treatise on "De Architectura Libra Decum". The eighth volume contains discussion about the sources and distribution of water.

CONCLUDING REMARKS

The earlier civilizations in the valleys of Indus, Tigris, Euphrates, Nile and Yellow rivers were using irrigation canals for supplying water for irrigation. In most of the cases these canals were unlined and they carried sediment; canals either took off from a weir or they were inundation canals. A frequent problem with these canals was silting and hence sediment removal was necessary. Locating the canal on the outer side of bend of a stream to reduce sediment entry into canal seems to have been practised. Chinese had made considerable progress in controlling large rivers, flood diversion and similar other processes. Records do not show the methods used for design of unlined channels. The Romans had made significant progress during this perioed in water supply to cities and in sewerage. Records also indicate that the Greeks knew about changing settling velocities of different particles and used the principle of decantation.

Chapter 3

Developments During 1600–1800 A.D.

During 1600–1800 A.D. relatively more progress was made in understanding the flow in alluvial rivers. During this period major activity took place in Europe and in this endeavour engineers, mathematicians, scientists and even a physician made notable contributions. There was an emphasis on experimentation to study certain phenomena under consideration; equally, analytical abilities were used to study the physics of the problem. As a result, this period can be considered to be the period of beginning of Fluvial Hydraulics.

CONTRIBUTION OF GUGLIELMINI

The first engineer whose contributions during the period 1600–1800 are worth mentioning is Dominico Guglielmini (1655–1710), a hydraulician and a physician born in 1655, who was employed in Venice and other Italian cities to prepare plans for the solutions of river problems there. His most important work was the building of levees on the river Po above Plaisance. His book "Della Natura di Flumi Trattato Fisico Mathematico" was published in Bologna in 1697. Guglielmini's experience was obtained more by field observations than by laboratory experiments. His major observations as regards river hydraulics can be summarised as follows (111, 197, 239).

Dominico Guglielmini (1655-1710)

He realised that the velocity distribution in the vertical is not uniform. According to him, "greater the quantity of water a river carries, the less will be its fall; and, greater the force of the stream, the less will be the slope of its bed." His writing indicates that Guglielmini had a notion of resistance of the bed to the flow. He had also realised the importance of depth of flow and channel slope in the phenomena of scour and deposition which later crystalised into a shear stress parameter. Further, he also stated that for scour to take place, it becomes necessary that the "scouring force" is greater than the "resistance of the soil". Guglielmini had a notion of size reduction of bed sediment along the river length. He believed that the fine material found near the lower ends of most of the rivers was produced by pulverising of the coarse material in the bed by grinding together of the fragments as they moved along the stream. His writings further indicate that he was the first to realise the existence of the condition of equilibrium between tendency of water to increase its velocity as it flowed down the plane and the opposition action of bed resistance.

While some of the statements made by Guglielmini in his book have been proved to be incorrect in the light of present day knowledge of the subject, on the whole his work was a remarkable achievement.

The second distinguished pioneer in this field during the above mentioned period was Paul Frizi born in 1727. Frizi, who was professor of mathematics at Milan, published in 1762 the first edition and in 1767 the second edition of his treatise on "Rivers and Torrents with the Method of Regulating Their Courses and Channels". This book was later translated into English by Maj. Gen. John Garstin and published in London in 1818. Frizi discussed a variety of problems related to river improvement and transportation of solids by flowing water. He gave the first account of laboratory experiments for studying such problems. Frizi did not agree with the concept of pulverisation of sediment particles by their impact on each other in a river along its length. To prove this point he placed a number of rock fragments in a box, and shook it for a long time, noting that the reduction in weight which resulted was only a small part of the total. Both Guglielmini and Frizi were probably unaware of the sorting phenomenon.

Frizi also stated that the amount of agitation i.e. (the level of turbulence) necessary to keep the particles fully mixed with flow (i.e. in suspension) would depend on the mass of the particle. This indicates a qualitative understanding of the turbulent nature of the flow and its role in keeping the sediment in suspension.

Both Guglielmini and Frizi stated their rules regarding transportation of sediment in terms of discharge and slope.

The German engineer Albert Brahms (1692–1758) was born in Sande, in the vicinity of Wilhemshaven and grew in the farming community (84). He was well versed in geography, mathematics and languages and used this knowledge in solving hydraulic problems. Brahms wrote a book titled "Anfangsgrunde der Deich und Wasser-Bankunst" which was published at Hanover in 1757. In this book, he empirically obtained a simple law for beginning of sediment motion on the channel bed. This law gives the proportionality between the bed velocity u_b

(i.e., flow velocity near the bed) and submerged weight of the particle W' under incipient motion as

$$u_b \sim W'^{1/6} \tag{1}$$

At about the same time the French engineer Pierre Louis Du Buat (1734–1809) wrote a two-volume treatise on "Principes d'Hydraulique" in 1786. His second volume of the treatise presents experimental data on resistance to flow in channels and pipes of various sizes and shapes. On the basis of such studies he proposed a resistance law of the form

Pierre Louis Du Buat (1734–1809)

$$U = \frac{49R - 0.8}{\sqrt{1/S} - \ln\sqrt{1/S + 16}} - 0.05\sqrt{R} \tag{2}$$

where U is the average velocity of flow, R is the hydraulic radius and S is the channel slope. Later R. Woltman (1754–1837), after studying Du Buat's work, suggested a simpler equation

$$U = C_W \sqrt{RS} \tag{3}$$

which is similar to Chezy's equation. Here C_w is Woltman's coefficient. Analysing Du Buat's data, Johann Albert Eytelwein (1764–1848) another German engineer, proposed the relation

$$U = 50.9\sqrt{RS} \tag{4}$$

in 1801. Du Buat also conducted experiments on the velocities necessary to move sediment particles of seven types ranging from clay to egg sized stones. The experiments were conducted in a 0.48 m wide and 43 m long flume. Velocity near the bed was determined by timing red currants over a distance of 20 m. Since currants were only slightly heavier than water, they moved freely close to the bed and gave the bottom velocity. Surface velocities were determined by floats and noting the time required for the float to travel 20 m. His results as summarised by Leliavsky (184), and Mavis *et al.* (196, 197) are given in Table 1.

The following quotation from Du Buat's treatise as given by Graf (111), indicates vividly Du Buat's keen observation and understanding of some phenomena in Fluvial Hydraulics:

> "The way running water attacks the bed which cannot resist any more and how the sand is shoved is facinating indeed, and deserves description. At times, it is an eddy which carries with it the soil and the fine sand, like the wind might carry the smoke, and this happens when the velocity is strong enough such that the impact of the water overcomes the inertia of the solid

particles. At other times, it is smooth and so to speak methodic working, which one may call a major work of dynamics. I shall try to describe this.

TABLE-1: Scour Velocities Obtained by Du Buat (184,196,197)

No.	Description	Scouring Velocity(cm/s)
1.	Potter's clay	10.6
2.	Coarse sand	21.6
3.	Gravel and sand taken from Seine river	
	Size of aniseed	10.8
	Size of peas	18.9
	Size of marsh plants beans	32.5
4.	Size of pebbles about an inch in diameter or more	65.0
5.	Sharp edged flint of the size of an egg or larger (Relative density 2.54-2.64)	96.0

When the bottom velocity is large enough to bring a body of a specific weight exceeding the one of water into motion and to transport it, then those bodies (particles) do not move uniformly, but much rather they tramp and jump. Take for example the sand.

Suppose the channel bed is made up of sand of the size to be distinguished by eyes, and suppose the velocity is found to be 10 to 12 "pouces" (inches) per second, then the channel bed appears like the pattern of a tapestry, which is known under the name Hungarian, such that irregular furrows appear whose direction is perpendicular to the water course.

Each of these furrows has two glacis with opposing slopes; the one which faces the water has a long slope, and has a common summit with the one which opposes the water and is much steeper and lies downstream. The profile of a furrow resembles the one of the glacis and of a covered walkway at a fortification. At about a distance of a foot from the steep slope begins a gentle one of another furrow, and this is repeated going downstream. A grain pushed by the current, moves up the gentle slope of the first talus, arrives at the summit, and rolls down due to its weight along the opposing slope; here in the shelter of the fluid's action it pauses and will be covered by other grains which arrived the same way. This work resembles the one of a ditch-digger who takes his wheel barrow up the ramp to unload it and the soil tumbles into the depth. The sand grains thus buried, remain there loaded down and covered by other ones until the total mass of the furrow, which they have left behind, has passed over them. It is thus that the entire furrow deplaces itself and advances little by little for its own width. Thus, the particle under consideration appears at the beginning of the new slope which was just created, and since it is again exposed to the influence of the current, it climbs the slope and falls then into the depth just as it did the first time. All of the furrows move very slowly, and for moderate water velocity it may take no less than an hour that everyone progresses by 4 to 5 pouces (inches). When water velocity increases, this activity increases too, but decreases, however, as soon as the one diminishes. Under average work, two years are required for a sand grain to travel a distance of 2400 toises....."

A brief description of armouring of channel has also been given.

"Since the smallest sand and clay becomes removed most easily, we find on the channel bed the most coarse sand, pebbles, stones, and other large objects which tumble upon it and remain there. They often give the stream bed such a strength that the resistance of it causes the stream to widen its bed or it might change it altogether, if it meets to the right and to the left less resistance...."

Thus it can be seen that Du Buat was aware of the intermittency of sediment movement, role of turbulent eddies, formation of bed undulations and their downward movement, and armouring process.

That the same rate of flow should occur for successive sections of flow, in the case of steady flow conditions, was recognised earlier by Frontinus (40–103) who was connected with the water supply of Rome. Leonardo Da Vinci (1452–1519), an Italian by birth—who showed equal genius in painting, drawing, sculpture, music, philosophy, botany, geology, engineering, and architecture indicated in his writings that he clearly understood this principle of continuity. The proportionality $Q \sim AU$ was fully recognised by Benedetta Castelli (1577–1644) in his book "Della Misura Delle Acque Correnti" in 1628. d'Alembert (1717–1783) gave the differential equation for continuity which was generalised by Leonhard Euler (1707–1783) and presented in the form

$$\frac{\partial \rho_f}{\partial t} + \frac{\partial (\rho_f u)}{\partial x} + \frac{\partial (\rho_f v)}{\partial y} + \frac{\partial (\rho_f w)}{\partial z} = 0 \qquad (5)$$

It was also during this period that the equations of motion for inviscid fluids were obtained by Euler. The equations, now known as Euler's equations of motion, are

$$\left.\begin{aligned}
\frac{\partial u}{\partial t} + u\frac{\partial u}{\partial x} + v\frac{\partial u}{\partial y} + w\frac{\partial u}{\partial z} &= X - \frac{1}{\rho_f}\frac{\partial p}{\partial x}\\
\frac{\partial v}{\partial t} + u\frac{\partial v}{\partial x} + v\frac{\partial v}{\partial y} + w\frac{\partial v}{\partial z} &= Y - \frac{1}{\rho_f}\frac{\partial p}{\partial y}\\
\frac{\partial w}{\partial z} + u\frac{\partial w}{\partial x} + v\frac{\partial w}{\partial y} + w\frac{\partial w}{\partial z} &= Z - \frac{1}{\rho_f}\frac{\partial p}{\partial z}
\end{aligned}\right\} \qquad (6)$$

where u, v, w are the velocity components in x, y, z directions respectively, ρ_f is the mass density of fluid, p is the pressure, and X, Y, Z are the components of body force per unit mass, in the three directions respectively.

Earlier, Daniel Bernoulli (1700–1782) had initiated the concept of principle of conservation of pressure energy, kinetic energy and potential energy in fluids. However, what is now known as Bernoulli s equation, was rigorously derived by Euler.

The credit for giving not only the first, but also the most lasting resistance formula goes to the French engineer Antonie Chez'y (1718–1798). In analysing the problem of supplying water from the river Yvette to Paris, Chez'y found that not enough information was available to determine the channel cross-section for providing a certain discharge. In analysing this problem he assumed that the resisting force due to friction will be proportional to PU^2 where P is the perimeter; on the other hand the gravitational force will be proportional to AS where A is the cross sectional area and S is the channel slope. Hence, if we have two channels, one can write

$$\frac{P_1 U_1^2}{A_1 S_1} = \frac{P_2 U_2^2}{A_2 S_2} \quad \text{or} \quad U_2 = U_1 \sqrt{\frac{R_2 S_2}{R_1 S_1}}$$

where R represents the hydraulic radius. It was only later that the constant of proportionality was included and Chez'y's equation was written as

$$U = C\sqrt{RS} \tag{7}$$

As regards size analysis of sediments, there is a reference which indicates (168) that in 1671 sieves were used in mining of tinstone. However, Van Leeuwenhoek seems to have used sieves for the first time in 1704 for scientific investigation of sediments. In 1769, Eller used sedimentation and showed that sands settled first and finer components formed their layer above it. During the latter part of 18th century, scientists in Europe used methods of sedimentation and decantation in separating particles of different sizes. In this connection details of works of Schroter 1774, Linne 1777, Wiegleb 1784, Ruckert 1789-90 can be seen (168).

CONCLUDING REMARKS

During this period, significant progress was made in formulating the basic equations governing the flow, namely the continuity equation and equations of motion. However, the friction term in the equations of motion was not included in the case of real fluid flows. Energy equation was also available. As regards Fluvial Hydraulics concept of critical or incipient motion condition was introduced and was expressed either in terms of bottom shear or velocity near the bed. Resistance law, presumably valid for rivers, was given by Woltman, Eytelwein, and Chez'y. The notions of sediment suspension, reduction of bed material size along the length, armouring and bed undulations were introduced but no quantitative information was available. Lastly, books on rivers and river hydraulics were made available.

Chapter 4

Developments During 19th Century

Relatively much more progress was made in understanding movement of water and sediment in the rivers as well as in understanding laws of fluid motion during 19th century. Most of the contributions during this period were made by the French, German, Italian, British and Belgian engineers. For the sake of convenience of discussion, these contributions can be grouped under the following heads:

- Incipient Motion
- Sediment Transport
- Sediment Measurements and Samplers
- Channel Resistance
- Rivers and Channels
- Equations of Motion and Similarity

INCIPIENT MOTION

During the 19th century, studies were conducted by several investigators about the beginning of motion of particles on the bed. Here the beginning of motion was related to the bottom (or near bed velocity) or surface velocity. The sediment size was many times described qualitatively and sometimes quantitatively. Findings of Bouniceau 1845, Blackwell (as quoted in 129) 1857, Gras (112) 1857 and Lechalas (182) 1871 and Suchier, 1874 can be briefly mentioned. Gras argued that a pebble on the bottom of a channel is displaced by the impulse of filaments which strikes it, and that the movement will take place when the velocity of these filaments exceeds the critical speed limit of traction. According to him the critical speed or competent velocity depends on the density, volume and form of the pebbles, on the density of the fluid and the depth of flow. On this premise he tried to explain how a non-saturated stream tends to become saturated, and in doing so, tends to select its materials from the finer grain sizes.

Lechalas distinguished between transportation of solids by traction (i.e. as bed-load) and in suspension. Lechalas attributed suspension to the action of eddies and vortices. He assumed that tractive force was proportional to the square of velocity for given sediment characteristics. For the Loire river sand he assumed critical mean velocity $U_{cr} = 0.25$ m/s and gave the following relations for velocity of bed waves.

$$\left.\begin{aligned} U_w &= 0.00037\,(U_{cr}^2 - 0.06), \quad \text{for } 0.25 < U_{cr} < 0.55 \text{ m/s} \\ U_w &= 0.00037\,U_{cr}^2, \quad \text{for } U_{cr} > 0.55 \text{ m/s} \end{aligned}\right\} \qquad (8)$$

From his observations on the Loire in France, Sainjon (as given in 224) deduced the following empirical equation for the velocity of bed undulations U_w,

$$U_w = 0.00013\,(u_s^2 - 0.11) \qquad (9)$$

where u_s is the surface velocity. D.F. Deacon (as given in 184) conducted experiments in 1892 in a flat bottomed trough with glass sides. It was found that the first movement of isolated sand particles occurred when surface velocity was 0.4 m /s. The ripples formed at this velocity. The ripple velocity U_w and surface velocity u_s observed by Deacon are given below:

u_S m/s	U_W m/s
0.457	0.213
0.534	0.488
0.610	12.80
0.648	Saltation occurred
0.884	Ripples washed out

The results of these investigators are summarised by Mavis *et al.* (196) and are given in Table-2 on the next page. Here the velocities are in m/s.

It may also be mentioned that criterion for the beginning of sediment movement in the form $u_b \sim W'^{1/6}$ (*i.e.*, Brahm's law) was independently derived by W. Airy (184) in 1834.

In passing, it may be mentioned that the role of turbulent eddies in sediment movement and transportation was first emphasised by Partiot (224) in his article published in 1871. He found that sand of the Loire river was transmitted only intermittently in suspension, and that for most of the part it moved as bed-load except when there was great turbulence, in which case it was carried up until it reached the surface.

TABLE-2: Critical velocities obtained by different investigators (196)
(Relative Density 2.6 to 2.7)

	1	2	3	4
Size mm	Bouniceau	Blackwell	Sainjon	Suchier
Sand				
1/2				
C	0.305			
1				
V.C.				
2				
Granules	0.122		0.244	
4				
f		0.534–0.915		0.793
8				
m			0.488	0.915
16				
C	0.648			1.067–1.128
32				
V.C.	1.006	0.534–0.762	1.143	
		0.762–0.838		
64		0.838–0.915	1.494	1.463
		0.838–0.915		
128			2.012	1.799
256				

SEDIMENT TRANSPORT

A major step forward in fluvial Hydraulics was taken by the French engineer Paul Francois Dominique du Boys (1847 - 1924), who for the first time used average

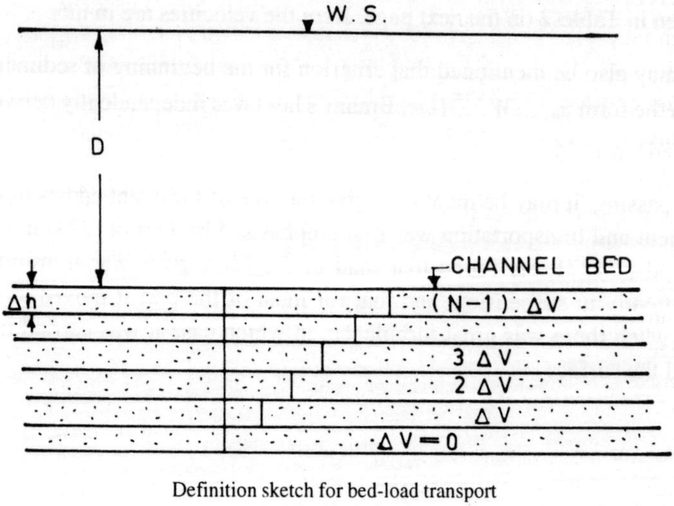

Definition sketch for bed-load transport

shear on the bed as the flow parameter. du Boys (57) 1879 argued that the force F exerted by the flow causing entrainment would be equal to the resistance of the bed or $F = \gamma_f DS$ per unit area where D is the depth of flow. Further, he assumed that the material on the bed moves in layers parallel to the bed, the velocity of the top layer being maximum and decreasing linearly for lower layers. If N layers are moving then the velocity of top layer will be $(N - 1)\,\Delta V$. Since the lowest layer is at rest the resisting force at that level must be equal to τ_0 or

$$\tau_0 = (\gamma_s - \gamma_f)\ N \cdot \Delta h \cdot \tan\phi$$

where Δh is the thickness of each layer, ϕ is the angle of internal friction, and γ_s and γ_f are the specific weights of sediment and water respectively. Hence

$$N = \tau_0 / \tau_c$$

where τ_c is critical shear when only top layer will be in motion. Further, the rate of bed-load transport in weight per unit width is

$$q_B = N \cdot \gamma_s \Delta h \cdot (N - 1)\frac{\Delta V}{2}$$

Combining these equations one get

$$\left.\begin{aligned} q_B &= A\tau_0(\tau_0 - \tau_c) \\ \text{where} \quad A &= \gamma_s \cdot \Delta h \cdot \Delta V / 2\tau_c^2 \end{aligned}\right\} \qquad (10)$$

The derivation given here indicates the unrealistic assumptions made by du Boys in obtaining expression for q_B. For example, it has been observed that at any given time, particles in the thickness of only one or two particle diameters are in motion. Also du Boys assumes, implicitly, that bed is always plane whereas it can be undulated also. However, in spite of these limitations, this form of equation for q_B has been found to be essentially correct and used by several later investigators.

SEDIMENT MEASUREMENTS AND SAMPLERS (137, 168)

Although much practical knowledge regarding sediment was obtained by earlier civilisations, as discussed earlier, as far as our knowledge of size analysis and suspended sediment sampling methods are concerned, the history does not go back more than two centuries.

It was in the beginning of 19th century that the word "mechanical analysis" of sediment was introduced in literature by Fleuriau-Bellevue in 1800. In 1830, G. Schübler established the first grade sizes in terms of actual dimensions and expressed the result of sediment analysis in percent. W.L. Rham in 1840 carried out an analysis using a set of three sieves in conjunction with decantation. F. Schulze developed the first elutriator in 1839 and made significant contribution to the problem of mechanical analysis as well as he did much to pave the way for further refinements. After Stokes' law for settling of spherical particle was developed in 1850, more emphasis was laid on using hydraulic methods for size analysis. E. Schöne in 1867 introduced the concept of characterising particles by fall velocity rather than size, shape, relative density, etc. W.R. Williams in 1895 gave a classification of sediment particles ranging from stones (greater than 10 mm diameter) through gravel (10 mm-3 mm), sand (3 mm - 0.25 mm), dust (0.25 mm - 0.0015 mm), to clay (less than 0.0015 mm). In 1895, Snyder used a centrifuge in the analysis. The same technique was used by C.G. Hopkins in 1899. J.A. Udden in 1898 established the geometric grade-scale which is essentially the same as that now in general use in the USA. His grades ranged from coarse gravel (8 mm - 4 mm diameter) to very fine dust (1/128 mm - 1/256 mm) in such a manner that the diameters of the largest particles in one grade have twice the diameter of the coarsest particles in the next finer grade.

The first suspended sediment samples were taken by Gorsse and Subuors (137) on the Rhine river in France in 1808 and 1809. Blohm (137) sampled the Elbe river at Hamburg, Germany from 1837-1854 and concluded that the concentration was uniform throughout the depth. The earliest samples on the Mississippi were collected by Captain Talcott of the US Army in 1838 but no record is kept of the sampling method used. The first known computations in Europe of the amount of sediment carried by the stream over a period of year were made by M. Baumgarten (18) on the Garonne river in France in 1839 to 1846. However, in India, R. Everest (79) measured the soluble and insoluble solids in the Ganges river between July and October 1831. In this paper, he has also mentioned about the measurements earlier made by Captain Forbes on the Ganges. Probably Forshey (275) was the first to collect samples on the Mississippi at Carrollton (Louisiana), USA in 1851 when samples at three verticals and three samples in each vertical were taken on a routine basis. The depth integrated samples were probably taken for the first time by A. Cunningham (51) on the Ganga canal in India during 1874-1879 using a vertical pipe extending to the full depth. The depth integration, accomplished by means of a sampler moving between the surface and the bottom, and taking a part of the sample from each depth, seems to have been first used in 1897 by the US Geological Survey (137) in the Rio Grande river.

A brief discussion about development of suspended sediment samplers is in order. In the earlier sediment investigations in the European rivers, in the beginning of 19th century, a can or a container was used; it was dipped in the stream and a "near surface" sample was collected. An ordinary bucket was used by the earliest investigators in the Mississippi river in the USA, around 1840. A keg sampler (137) was used by Forshey in the Mississippi at Carrollton, USA in 1851. It was a small weighed keg equipped with a flap valve at each end. As it was lowered, the keg was maintained in the vertical and the flap valves were opened upwards due to the reaction of water; they were closed when the sampler was halted at a desired depth. This sampler was improved by J.B.Johnson during the investigations on the Mississippi in 1879. The flaps were held in open position by a catch mechanism which operated and closed the flaps when the trigger mechanism below the sampler touched the stream bed.

Vertical pipe in the form of depth integrating sampler was used by Cunningham in 1874-1879 in the Ganga canal by pushing 12 ft (3.66 m) length of a vertical pipe downwards through the stream. The pipe was closed at its lower end by a movable lid actuated by a spring.

A "slip bottle" used in the Missouri and the Mississippi rivers in 1880 - 1881 was the first of the instantaneous trap samplers. This consisted of an iron cylinder 20 cm in diameter and 15 cm long which moved along a vertical concentric rod. Two iron discs were fastened to the rod, separated by a distance equal to the height of the cylinder, the upper disc acting as the piston inside the cylinder in the closed position.

CHANNEL RESISTANCE (239)

During 19th century, further progress was made in the development of resistance law for pipes and open channels. Julius Weisbach, (1806-1871), who taught applied mathematical sciences at the Friberg School of Mines was the first to write the resistance equation for pipes in the form

$$h_f = f\frac{L}{D}\frac{U^2}{2g} \tag{11}$$

where h_f is the head loss in a length L, D is the pipe diameter, U is the average velocity of flow in the pipe and f is what is now called Darcy-Weisbach friction factor. Weisbach found f to vary not only with U but also with pipe diameter and nature of wall material (i.e its surface roughness).

Assistant of Darcy at Dujon, Henri Emile Bazin (1829-1917), along with Darcy conducted a large number of tests on trapezoidal, rectangular and semicircular channels made of cement, wood, brick, gravel and rock with the purpose of determining the relationship between hydraulic radius R, slope S and velocity U. Their data indicated

$$RS = \left(a + \frac{b}{R}\right) U^2 \tag{12}$$

whereas earlier R.D. Prony had obtained

$$RS = \left(a' + \frac{b'}{U}\right) U^2 \tag{13}$$

They found that a and b varied with S in such a manner that $a \sim S$ and $b \sim \frac{1}{S}$ but $\left(a + \frac{b}{R}\right)$ remained nearly constant.

In the USA, Captain A.A.Humphreys and Lieutenant H.L.Abbott in 1861 submitted a "Report upon the Physics and Hydraulics of the Mississippi River" in connection with controlling the Mississippi floods. They used the Mississippi river data to verify the formulae then existing in Europe and on failure to do so they devised a new and cumbersome formula. The two Swiss engineers Emile Oscar Ganguillet (1818-1894) and Wilhelm Rudolph Kutter (1818-1888), applied

Humphreys and Abbott's formula to Swiss rivers. They found that neither Bazin nor Humphreys-Abbott formula was good enough and hence recommended a new formula

$$C = \frac{a + \dfrac{b}{N} + \dfrac{m}{S}}{1 + \left(a + \dfrac{m}{S}\right)\dfrac{N}{\sqrt{R}}} \tag{14}$$

for Chezy's C. Here a, b and m are constants and N depends on the roughness of the surface, varying three fold for the six surfaces studied. Philippe Gascard Gauckler (1826-1905), engineer at Ponts et Chaussées, France, proposed two formulae for U in 1868, namely

$$\left.\begin{aligned} U &= \lambda_1 R^{4/3} S \quad \text{if } S > 0.0007 \\ U &= \lambda_2 R^{2/3} S^{1/2} \quad \text{if } S < 0.0007 \end{aligned}\right\} \tag{15}$$

It may be noticed that the second formula has the same structure as Manning's equation proposed later.

An Irish engineer Robert Manning (1816-1897), at one time President of the Institution of Civil Engineers (Ireland), was primarily a hydrologist. In 1889, he published a paper titled,"On the Flow of Water in Open Channels and Pipes", in which he proposed the relationship

$$U = K R^{2/3} S^{1/2} \tag{16}$$

Apparently he was unware of Gauckler's work. However, he did not suggest that Kutter's $N = 1/K$.

It can thus be seen that the three most popular forms of resistance relationship, namely Darcy-Weisbach, Chez'y, and Manning were established by the end of 19th century. It was also realised that the roughness coefficient was dependent on the scale of surface roughness and velocity. However, these parameters were not put in dimensionless forms. Further, in case of alluvial rivers it was known that bed undulations form in the river; however their exact role in resistance was not known.

At the end of 19th century, it was realised that presence of suspended load may reduce the resistance to flow. A. Flamont in 1891 commenting on the work of Duponchee (as quoted in 36) said," It appears from these experiments as if, other things being equal, the mean velocity of water charged with silt is greater than that of clear water." Also an anonymous writer in "Indian Engineering" in 1892 - quoted by Lindley in his discussion on Buckley's paper (36) concluded from 3800 observations on seven channels, that Kutter's N decreased with increase of silt content. This aspect was later investigated by Gilbert, Buckley, Vanoni, and others.

RIVERS AND CHANNELS

In the latter half of 19th century some progress was made in the understanding of flow in alluvial rivers and channels.The foremost among those who contributed to the understanding of alluvial rivers was O. Fargue (1827-1910), a French engineer who was working at Ponts et Chaussées. Fargue (46) was closely associated with the developmental work on the Garonne river. On the basis of observations on the Garonne, he gave a system of rules which later became quite popular in Europe. These rules (184) are as follows:

1. The thalweg of the river tends always towards the concave bank of the river; silt and sand, on the other hand, are deposited in the form of beaches or wide-shores, on the opposite convex bank.
2. The depth of the pool, at the concave bank, and width of the low sandy beach on the convex side, both increase with the curvatures of respective banks.
3. Their maxima do not coincide.The deepest spot of the river channel and the greatest width of the beach are somewhat behind the point of greatest curvature.A similar lag is observed between the inflexion point and the crest of the corresponding bar.
4. The stability of the eroded channel as well as its smoothness depend on the gradual variation of curvature. Abrupt changes in the radius of curvature cause undesirable disturbance and irregularities of channel formation.
5. These laws hold good only where the ratio of channel width to length of meander is neither too great, nor too small.

From the analysis of observations on the Garonne, Fargue proposed the following empirical relation between radius of the bend R and the mean depth in the bend D_m, both in m.

$$1/R = 0.03\,D_m^3 - 0.23\,D_m^2 + 0.78\,D_m - 0.76 \qquad (17)$$

It can be seen that it is a purely geometric relationship and does not include terms involving sediment transport and another flow parameters on which R and D_m should depend.

Two other contributions on the bends during this period are those of J. Boussinesq. In his publication "Essai sur la Theorie des Eaux Courantes" published in 1872, he gave an expression for additional slope S_1 required in a bend. His expression is

$$S_1 = \frac{\alpha}{D}\sqrt{\frac{B}{R}}\,U^2 \qquad (18)$$

where B and D are width and depth of flow, R the radius of bend and $\alpha = 0.0003$ to 0.0005. He further obtained expression for the average depth in the bend D_m as

$$\frac{D_m}{D} = \left(1 + \frac{\alpha}{\beta}\sqrt{B/R}\right) \qquad (19)$$

where $\beta = 0.00036$. Lastly, J. Thompson (265) in 1876, observed the transverse circulation induced in a bend in a series of experiments in 180 degrees open channel bend. The spiral motion was observed using seeds and anilin dye. Also N. de Leliavsky (207) 1894, developed an instrument for measuring the transverse components of velocity in spiral motion.

By the end of 19th century a paper was published by R.G. Kennedy (158) 1895, on stable channel design which later formed the basis of research on the subject in India and abroad for the next six decades or so. Robert Gregg Kennedy (1851-1920) was born in the UK (43) in 1851; he attended the Royal Indian Engineering College and then joined as an irrigation engineer in India in 1873. He was promoted as executive engineer in 1887, when he studied the conditions of alluvial channels running in fairly stable or regime condition. He made observations on a portion of the main canal of Upper Bari Doab canal network and about 150 km of the lower reach. The discharges in the main canal and tributaries ranged from about 1.0 m^3/s to 50 m^3/s. On the basis of data from 30 sitess where the canals were in stable or regime condition, he found that the velocity U_0 is related to depth D of the flow as

$$U_0 = 0.55\, D^{0.64} \qquad (20)$$

in mks units. These canals had different width/depth ratios. Kennedy called U_0 as critical or nonscouring — nonsilting velocity. If the velocity is less than U_0, deposition of sediment would occur and if it is greater, scouring is expected. Kennedy recognised that the nonsilting — nonscouring velocity would depend on the bed material size and sediment concentration; however, the effect of the latter was neglected and the effect of sediment size was incorporated by replacing 0.55 by 0.55m. The coefficient m, known as the critical velocity ratio, is greater than unity for the bed material coarser than that found in Upper Bari Doab canal system, and less that unity for the material finer than that. He also stated that if the canal carries a sediment concentration of $\bar{C}_s$ at a velocity of U and depth D, the amount of sediment deposited will be $\bar{C}_s\,(1 - (U/U_0)^{5/2})$. Later various investigators found that the constant in Eq. (20) varies appreciably from one canal system to the other, which is partly due to omission of the concentration effect on the coefficient. Kennedy suggested the use of Chezy's equation with Ganguillet-Kutter formula for determining C using N as 0.0225 in the formula. According to him, a canal can be designed for known Q, N, S, m and the side slopes. Kennedy realised that some reationship for channel width either as a function of depth or discharge was also necessary to design a channel which is stable, since a narrow and deep as well as wide and shallow channels cannot be equally stable; however, he could not recommend such a relationship.

Kennedy did not make further studies to improve and generalise his formula; this could be partly due to the fact that he was entrusted with more technical administrative responsibilities. He became Joint Secretary to the Punjab Irrigation Department in 1904, and Secretary for Irrigation to the Chief Commissioner of the

North West Frontier Provinces in 1905. He retired from the service in 1906 and was nominated as Companion (of the order) of the Indian Empire (CIE) in 1907. He died in 1920.

During the fag end of 19th century British engineers working on large alluvial rivers in the Indo-Gangetic plain made significant contribution in evolving a method of building bridges and weirs in contracted portions of the river. Two names which deserve mention in this regard are Francis J.E.Spring and J.R.Bell. Spring who started working on large Indian rivers around 1870 was either associated with or was in charge of design and construction of bridges on the Chenab, Krishna, Godavari, Mahanadi and other rivers, and was involved with the design of river training works for these rivers and the Brahmaputra.

They evolved a method of training of large rivers so that in spite of their wandering or meandering tendency, they may pass through and not outflank road and railway bridges or irrigation weir built across them. Spring (258) 1903, suggested a method to assess the extent of constriction that can be done with rivers flowing through coarse, medium, fine and very fine sandy material. The method proposed by Gales (87) 1938, makes use of the river section at the bend in flood to assess the extent to which the section of the bridge can be advantageously allowed to develop. By reducing the length to 20 to 25 per cent of original width of river,

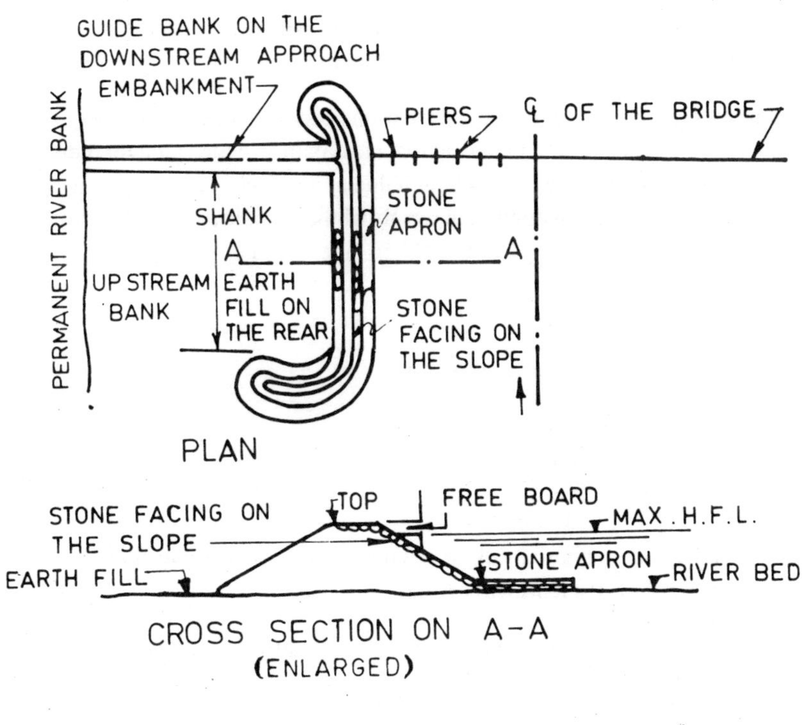

Typical guide bund

the cost of structure is significantly reduced. In order to ensure that the river continues to flow through the narrow section and does not outflank the bridge, guide bunds on both sides were proposed and their design evolved. Basic principles on the basis of which length of guide bunds, radii of curvature of heads of guide bunds, stone pitching and launching apron are to be designed were also mentioned. Typical guide bund is shown in the adjoining sketch.

It may also be mentioned that in 1875 Fargue built the first known movable bed model of the Garonne river at Bordeaux, France. The model was undistorted one with length scale of 1:100, and the time and velocity scales were arbitrarily chosen. Nevertheless, it was reported that the model was used with appreciable success (54, 239). The idea of building distorted model was also conceived at the end of 19th century. Osborne Reynolds built a tidal river model with a distortion of three; sand was placed on the bottom to see the effect of currents.

In order to complete the discussion on models and model laws, the contribution of William Froude (1810-1879), needs to be mentioned (239). He used similarity law of Reich for predicting the resistance of prototype ships from model tests. He also conducted experiments on the skin friction of submerged planks in length varying from 3.0 m to 15.0 m with different roughnesses, with the object of determining the variation of resistance with velocity, length and surface roughness. These experiments and results therefrom indicated that he had the idea of continued effect of viscosity in retarding the flow over these surfaces with the increase in length—the basis of boundary layer development.

Another significant contribution during this period is due to Sternberg (259) who in 1875 developed a mathematical model to obtain an expression for reduction of bed material in a stream along its length due to attrition. The analysis is based on the assumption that the reduction in weight of the particle dW is proportional to its weight W and the distance travelled dL ; in other words

$$dW = -\alpha W dL \quad (21)$$

where α is a coefficient. Its integration gives

$$W / W_0 = e^{-\alpha L}$$

or

$$d / d_0 = e^{-\alpha L/3} \quad (22)$$

where W_0 and d_0 are the initial weight and diameter of the particle at $L = 0$ and W and d the corresponding quantities at $L = L$.

Thus by the end of 19th century a reasonably strong basis was laid to use analytical and experimental methods for studying flow in rivers. Importance of non-dimensional parameters such as friction coefficient f, Reynolds number Re and Froude number Fr was also recognised.

EQUATIONS OF MOTION AND SIMILARITY (239)

It was during this period that significant progress was also made in establishing the equations of motion and conditions of similarity of flows which later formed the basis of analysis of flows in alluvial streams.

Louis Marie Henri Navier (1785-1836), who was a native of Dijon, entered the Ponts et Chausse'es after academic training and taught at the Ecole Polytechnique and Ecole des Ponts et Chaussées, also simultaneously working with the Corps in Bridge Construction. During the same period he also continued his academic pursuits. In 1822 he submitted a paper to the Academie des Sciences, titled "Memoire sur les Lois due Movement des Fluides" in which he modified Euler's equations of motion by considering hypothetical attraction or repulsion between adjacent molecules. He expressed this force in terms of an unknown function of molelcular spacing and modified Euler's equations to

$$\rho_f \left(\frac{\partial u}{\partial t} + u\frac{\partial u}{\partial x} + v\frac{\partial u}{\partial y} + w\frac{\partial u}{\partial z} \right) = X - \frac{\partial p}{\partial x} + \varepsilon \left(\frac{\partial^2 u}{\partial x^2} + \frac{\partial^2 u}{\partial y^2} + \frac{\partial^2 u}{\partial z^2} \right) \quad (23)$$

etc. where ε represented simply a function of molecular spacing. Saint Venants (1797-1886) derived the above Navier's equations in 1843 on a more rational basis. In doing so he obtained expressions for the three normal and three tangential stresses in terms of velocity gradients, e.g.

$$\tau_{xx} = p + 2\varepsilon\frac{\partial u}{\partial x}, \quad \tau_{xy} = \varepsilon\left(\frac{\partial u}{\partial y} + \frac{\partial v}{\partial x}\right), \quad \tau_{xz} = \varepsilon\left(\frac{\partial u}{\partial z} + \frac{\partial w}{\partial x}\right), \text{ etc.}$$

The British mathematician Sir Gorge Gabriel Stokes (1819 - 1903), who was a native of Skreen, Ireland, received his education at Cambridge and remained in England contributing to the theoretical physics. In 1845, he wrote a paper "On the Theories of Internal Friction of Fluids in Motion and of the Equilibrium and Motion of Elastic Solids". Herein he derived the equations of motion for fluids as they are derived presently by replacing ε by dynamic viscosity μ. Hence, the equations are known as Navier-Stokes equations. In 1862 he also obtained the equation for terminal fall velocity ω_0, of a small spherical particle of diameter d

$$\omega_0 = \frac{g\, d^2 (\rho_s - \rho_f)}{18\mu} = \frac{d^2}{18\,\mu}(\gamma_s - \gamma_f) \quad (24)$$

now known as Stokes' law. Here μ is the dynamic viscosity of fluid, ρ_s and ρ_f are the mass densities of sediment and fluid respectively, and d is the diameter of spherical particles. As shown later, Eq. 24 is valid when $(\omega_0\, d\, \rho_f / \mu)$ is less than 0.10 or 0.20.

The German physicist Gustav Robert Kirchhoff, (1824-1887), in 1873 presented to Berlin Academy of Sciences a dimensional analysis of the equations of fluid motion that gave similarity criteria as equality of Froude, Reynolds and Mach numbers.

Hagen, who had preceded Osborne Reynolds in demonstrating the existence of two types of flows namely laminar and turbulent, and Helmholtz had expressed the conditons for viscous-intertia similarity. However, it was Reynolds (1840-1912), in 1885 who formulated the parameter Reynolds number $\frac{UL\,\rho_f}{\mu}$ or $\frac{UD\,\rho_f}{\mu}$ and performed experiments to show that its limiting value, when flow changes from laminar to turbulent, is 1900-2000 for flow in pipes. Further in 1884, in a paper titled "On the Dynamic Theory of Incompressible Viscous Fluids and the Determination of the Criteria" he extended Navier-Stokes equations to the case of turbulant motion by introducing $u_i = \bar{u}_i + u_i'$ etc. and then retaining those terms in the equations which will have temporal mean values, other than zero. He showed that the resulting equations, known as Reynolds equations of motion, are:

$$\left.\begin{aligned} \rho_f \left(\frac{\partial \bar{u}}{\partial t} + \bar{u}\frac{\partial \bar{u}}{\partial x} + \bar{v}\frac{\partial \bar{u}}{\partial y} + \bar{w}\frac{\partial \bar{u}}{\partial z} \right) &= X - \frac{\partial \bar{p}}{\partial x} + u\left(\frac{\partial^2 \bar{u}}{\partial x^2} + \frac{\partial^2 \bar{u}}{\partial y^2} + \frac{\partial^2 \bar{u}}{\partial z^2} \right) \\ &\quad - \left(\frac{\partial (\rho_f \overline{u'^2})}{\partial x} + \frac{\partial (\rho_f \overline{u'v'})}{\partial y} + \frac{\partial (\rho_f \overline{u'w'})}{\partial z} \right) \end{aligned}\right\} \qquad (25)$$

Similar equations can be written in other two directions.

Mention may also be made of contributions of Giuseppe Venturoli, (1768-1846), and Jean Baptiste Belanger (1789-1874). Venturoli, professor of Applied Mathematics at the University of Bologna, Italy, first derived the elementary backwater equation for rectangular channels in 1823, even though with a wrong sign. Through graphical integration of the differential equation, he also plotted various branches of the surface profiles. However, his memoirs did not receive general circulation. Jean Baptiste Belanger, a native of Valenciennes, France, taught at many institutions including the Ecole des Ponts et Chaussées. He independently derived the elemenatary equation of backwater and published it in 1828. The equations of motion in open channels with friction term were known by the end of 19th century through the contributions of Navier-Stokes, Saints Venant, and Boussinesq. These formed the basic framework for the analysis of unsteady non-uniform flow in alluvial rivers in the latter half of 20th century.

CONCLUDING REMARKS

It can be seen that relatively good progress was made during 19th century in the development of Fluvial Hydraulics. As a result of experimental work,criterion for beginning of motion was developed in terms of average or bottom velocity. The concept of bed shear was used in the analysis and the first bed-load equation was developed. Sampling of streams for determination of sediment concentration was initiated in the beginning of the century and by the end of century, routine sampling with crude point and depth integrating samplers was done. The basic resistance laws, viz. those of Chez'y, Manning and Darcy-Weisbach, were developed and used and it was realised that the resistance coefficient for a given surface is not constant. In natural streams it was also noticed that it reduces with increase in sediment concentration. As regards flow in rivers, Fargue's rules on flow in bends were enunciated and the foundation for development of the regime method of channel design was established by the work of Kennedy. Also, methods of training of large rivers using guide bunds were developed in India. Lastly the basic equations of motion were developed which could later be used for studying the transient flows in rivers.

Chapter 5

Developments During 1900-1925

Relatively less progress was made in the first quarter of 20th century as far as Fluvial Hydraulics is concerned. During this period increasing use of the laboratory facilities was made to study sediment movement. The pioneering works of G.K.Gilbert, A. Schoklitsch, Gratz and F. Schaffernak can be mentioned in this respect. Further, more field data about stable channels and resistance were collected and analysed. Lastly, a beginning was made about using equations of motion to study formation and migration of bed undulations.

GILBERT'S CONTRIBUTION

The most significant contribution to Fluvial Hydraulics during the first quarter of 20th century came from Grove Karl Gilbert (1843-1918), a geologist by profession. Gilbert (194) was born in Rochester, N.Y. in 1843 where he studied in the University of Rochester and graduated at the age of nineteen. In 1869 he started working as a volunteer assistant to conduct a new survey of Ohio and continued working in this area until his death in 1918. Gilbert contributed significantly to the rise of a subscience, physiography (or geomorphology) describing the earth's surface and investigating the processes by which it is changed. Gilbert has been described (194) as "an authority in many fields and yet one who never assumed authority; a leader in science and yet one who never assumed leadership; neither power nor glory did he seek, but the satisfaction of contributing his share to the sum of human knowledge."

Grove Karl Gilbert
(1843–1918)

In 1884 Gilbert (106) described the sufficiency of earth's rotation for the deflection of streams leading to meandering. He pointed out that the deflective force due to terrestrial rotation varies directly with the velocity of the stream and he developed formulae to estimate the magnitude of this force. During the fag end of his career he did the most remarkable work of investigating flow of water over loose movable bed in laboratory flumes. This work was a consequence of protests and law suits following the spreading of mine waste over farms in the California's great central valley. The experiments were designed to determine, "the transport of debris" under changing conditions of water discharge, energy grade line and sediment properties. At Berkeley in California, Gilbert (107) conducted extensive experiments in three flumes with lengths 4.27 m, 9.6 m and 45.7 m, width varying between 0.07 m to 0.60 m, using discharges varying from 0.50 *l*/s to 34.0 *l*/s. Eight different sands were used with median diameter ranging from 0.305 mm to 7.01 mm and relative density between 2.53 and 2.69.

Gilbert gave a vivid description of the modes of sediment transportation. In this he observed the bouncing motion of sediment particles on the bed and it was called "saltation". He described formation of ripples and dunes at low rates of bed-load transport, the gradual disappearance of dunes and then the bed surface becoming flat. With further increase in flow a second rhythmic phase started in which a system of symmetric undulations travelled upstream; these were called antidunes. Their movement was accomplished by erosion on the downstream side and deposition on the upstream face. He found that the rate of sediment transport q_T varied as

$$\left.\begin{aligned} q_T &\sim (q - q_c)^{0.18 \text{ to } 1.24} \\ q_T &\sim (S - S_c)^{0.93 \text{ to } 2.37} \\ q_T &\sim \left(\frac{1}{d} - \frac{1}{d_c}\right)^{0.50 \text{ to } 0.62} \end{aligned}\right\} \tag{26}$$

in which q_c, S_c and d_c are the incipient motion values of unit discharge, channel slope and sediment size respectively. Gilbert did not attempt to develop a sediment transport relation and hence the results of his work were not available to practising engineers in the form of a formula. Apparently Gilbert did'nt believe that a transport relation based on the laboratory data could safely be extrapolated to the river conditions. Gilbert's data have been used by later investigators in developing predictors for regimes of flow, resistance and sediment transport.

It may be mentioned in passing that, as mentioned by Allen (6), Henry Clifton Sorby described many sedimentary structures in his paper published in 1859, and gave a tentative account of the mechanisms and hydraulics of several bed forms. J.S. Owen was probably the first to recognise in 1908, that a definite sequence of bed forms exists in a channel as one increases the discharge in the channel. This was confirmed by Gilbert in his experiments, V. Cornish in 1901, and Pierce in 1916, as mentioned by Allen (6), have described the formation of antidunes and the sequence through which the bed and the water surface pass.

SEDIMENT TRANSPORT

A large number of hydraulic laboratories were developed during the latter part of 19th century in Europe and they were very active in solving complex hydraulic problems faced by the engineers. Their facilities and summaries of research activities are described by Freeman (85). Some sediment problems were investigated in these laboratories during the period under consideration.

Armin Kart Kult Schoklitsch (84) was born in April 1988 in Walfau in Burgenland. After completing his studies in 1912, he worked with Phillip Forchheimer in Gratz till 1914 when he had to give up his academic work due to the first World War. He joined Gratz in 1920 again as lecturer and worked on experimental hydraulics. Between 1926 and 1940 he was engaged in the Technical Institute in Bruen, Czechoslovakia, and then between 1940 to 1945 he was called back in Gratz. After the second war was over he migrated to Argentina and worked as professor at the National University in Tucuman upto 1953 and then at Cuyo University in San Juan. He died in 1969 at San Juan in Argentina.

In the hydraulic laboratory at Gratz, Schoklitsch conducted experiments to study how sediment moved along bends and thereby confirm Fargue's rules. Experiments were also conducted in a rotating device to verify Sternberg's law of attrition, and the results did confirm the laws. Schoklistsch also conducted experiments on bed-load movement. He found that at no stage of experiments, a sliding of one layer over the other was observed as assumed by du Boys. However, for uniform sediments du Boy's law was verified. Schoklitsch conducted experiments with nonuniform sediment also. He found that for uniform as well as nonuniform sediments, the intensity of sediment movement is proportional to the product of shear and velocity at the particle level. He proposed bed-load equations of the form

$$\left.\begin{aligned} q_B &= \text{const.}\,(q - q_c) \\ \text{and} \quad q_B &= \text{const.}\,(D^{1.7} - D_c^{1.7}) \end{aligned}\right\} \tag{27}$$

where q_c and D_c are the critical discharge and depth at given slope and the constant depends on slope and sediment characteristics.

Experiments on location of intakes revealed that smallest amount of sediment entered the intake if it was located on the outer side of the bend. He also conducted experiments on reduction in fall velocity of sediment due to increase in concentration.

Friedrich Schaffernak who was in charge of the Experimental Institute for Hydraulic Engineering at Vienna, also devoted considerable efforts in the study of Fluvial Hydraulics. He conducted experiments in the laboratory for determining basic laws of transportation of sedimentary materials. Using sediments of natural size and composition, he prepared a graph between sediment size and critical bottom velocity, on which separate curves were obtained for different stages of motion viz. (i) oscillatory particle displacement, (ii) pieces of material thrown in

Friedrich Schaffernak
(1881–1951)

are carried, and (iii) beginning of movement of material initially at rest. His studies on sediment transportation revealed that du Boys equation is all right for uniform materials upto 10 mm size. For coarser materials a different relationship was proposed.

V.E. Timonoff in the hydraulics laboratory at Leningrad (St. Petersburg) conducted experiments for determining spacing of bridge piers in the case of parallel bridges. He also conducted scale model studies on the shoaling of the mouth of the river in Lake Tschudi. The horizontal and vertical scales of the model were 1:100 and 1:25 respectively and Buckwhite grit was used as the sediment.

STABLE CHANNELS

After publication of his paper in 1895, Kennedy in 1904 gave a rough rule for the ratio of bed width to depth of flow which would make the channel stable. It was suggested that this ratio should be between 3.5 and 7.0 for channels carrying discharge between 0.28 m^3/s and 28 m^3/s. In 1913 Garrett (103) prepared a set of hydraulic diagrams for designing non-silting and non-scouring channels, which were then widely used in India. In 1917 Wood published, in a tabular form, the computed results for the design of stable channels using Kennedy's method. During this period, in Egypt also equations similar to the one proposed by Kennedy were obtained. As discussed by Leliavsky (184), in Egyptian canals it was found that $U_0 \sim D^{0.67 \text{ to } 0.72}$

Further, it was found that depth, slope and bed width were related as

$$D = 0.10\ [0.50\,S + 0.40]\ \sqrt{B}$$

By 1919, Lindley (187) recognised that in stable channels there are three degrees of freedom i.e. width, depth and slope can adjust for given conditions. Hence, in addition to Kennedy type equation and Chezy's equation with Kutter's N, one additional relation for width is needed. On the basis of analysis of data from canals in Lower Chenab system, Lindley proposed

$$\left.\begin{aligned} U_0 &= 0.57\,D^{0.57} \\ B &= 7.8\,D^{0.61} \end{aligned}\right\} \qquad (28)$$

In reply to the discussion on his paper, Lindley stated that,"the existence of these relations meant that the dimensions, width, depth and gradient, of a channel to carry a given supply loaded with a given silt charge were all fixed by nature".

A few comments need to be made here. Firstly, these equations do not contain sediment load as one of the variables in design. Secondly, will different materials on the bed and side have the same influence on the above relationships? These and other aspects were considered later by Blench, and Simons and Albertson.

RIVER HYDRAULICS

Two aspects of River Hydraulics will be briefly discussed here. These are the resistance to flow and formation of dunes on the stream bed.

Albert Strickler
(1887–1963)

It was realised during the period under consideration that the Manning's n or Chezy's C would depend on the channel characteristics. Horton (130) 1916, proposed Kutter's N or Manning's n values depending on the channel description and on whether they were maintained under best, good, fair or bad conditions. The Manning's n varied from 0.025 to 0.15, a six fold change. Albert Strickler (1887-1963), who was a mechanical engineer and associated with the Technical Institute of Zurich, analysed (203) in 1923 the data from various streams in Switzerland which were flowing through coarse material with steep slopes and found that Manning's n_s is related to the median size d_{50} of bed material by the empirical relation

$$n_s = \frac{d_{50}^{1/6}}{21} \tag{29}$$

where d_{50} is in m. Under the stipulated conditions, bed will be devoid of any undulations and hence above equation would be valid for plane bed condition. Around the same time Schoklitsch (246) also attempted to relate n_s with the mean diameter of the surface layer. Through experimental work of Gilbert (107) it was realised that in alluvial streams bed undulations would influence the Manning's n significantly; but no attempt was made to explore the inter-relationship between resistance coefficient and either dimensions of undulations or the flow condition. However, attention was focussed on the effect of suspended load on the resistance.

Buckley (36) 1922, compared his current meter discharge measurements on the Nile with the formulae of Kutter, Bazin, and Manning, and found that these formulae gave velocities which were as much as 50 percent in error during the flood period when the suspended load concentration was high.

Indus River Commission Reports for the period 1906-1910 stated that at Kotri gauging station, the rising river had a higher velocity and discharge than the falling river for the same stage. Parker (223) 1925, also stated that, as a general rule, it may be stated that water which carries fine silt can be expected to show a somewhat lower value of n than clear water under similar conditions. On the other hand, Kanthack (36), in his discussion of Buckley's paper, quotes L.W.Collet, 1916. It was found that in the case of the Swiss rivers the mean velocity reduced very considerably with the increase of solid matter in suspension, the reduction in the velocity being attributed to the increased viscosity of water due to heavy charge of silt derived from schistose rocks. Similarly, Gilbert (107) felt that the streams are retarded by suspended sediment loads.

Buckley proposed the following formula for mean flow velocity

$$U = [147 + (\overline{C}_s - 10)^{0.383}]\, R^{0.85}\, S^{0.72} \tag{30}$$

where U is in m/s, R in m and $\overline{C}_s$ is the sediment concentration in ppm. Thus during this period there was a strong evidence to suggest that the friction decreased with increase in concentration in case of fine material whereas in the case of rivers with coarser material opposite effect was noticed. However, it was not realised that the bed formations can be a dominant factor which would increase the roughness and that the combined effect of suspended sediment and bed forms would finally decide whether friction is increased or decreased. This effect was later studies by Knapp, Vanoni and Nomicos.

It may be mentioned that Blasius (26) empasised the importance of Froude number $U/\sqrt{gD}$ in the bed-form analysis. For Fr greater than unity he observed diagonally placed bars while for Fr less than unity ripples and bars were observed.

The credit for providing a theoretical analysis for dune formation in alluvial streams goes to Exner (80) 1920. Exner showed that if in an alluvial channel transporting sediment, there is a small sinusoidal wave on the bed, it will gradually become unsymmetrical as it moves downstream and takes the form of an unsymmetrical dune. In the first simplified analysis he assumed water surface to be horizontal. If because of undulation on bed the flow is accelerated, the bed will scour if one assumes sediment transport capacity is dependent on U; for the conditions shown in the figure

$$\frac{\partial \eta}{\partial t} + \varepsilon \frac{\partial U}{\partial x} = 0 \tag{31}$$

where ε is called the erosion coefficent, see definition sketch. One can also write continuity equation for flow as

$$UB\,(Z - \eta) = Q = \text{const.} \tag{32}$$

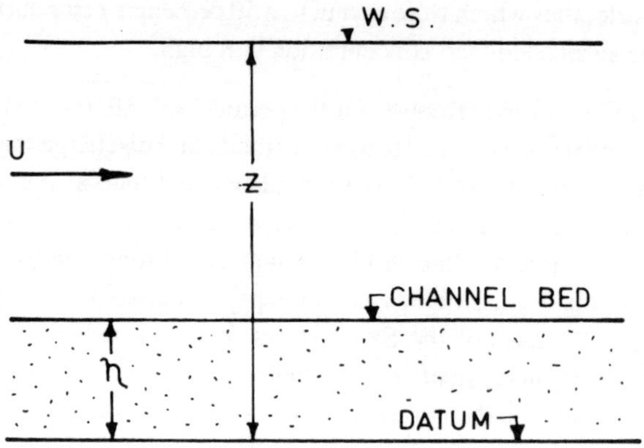

Definition sketch

where B is the channel width and Q is the discharge. Combining these two equations and assuming $\partial Z / \partial x = 0$, one gets

$$\frac{\partial Z}{\partial t} = -\frac{M}{(Z-\eta)^2}\frac{\partial Z}{\partial x} \text{ and } M = \varepsilon Q / B \tag{33}$$

General solution of Eq. (33) is

$$(Z-\eta) = f\left[\frac{Mt}{(Z-\eta)^2} - x\right] \tag{34}$$

where f is an arbitrarily chosen function. For example, if one assumes that at $t = 0$, bed profile is given as

$$\eta = A_0 + A_1 \cos \alpha x \tag{35}$$

for any time t one gets

$$\eta = A_0 + A_1 \cos \alpha \left(x - \frac{Mt}{(Z-\eta)^2}\right) \tag{36}$$

The profile plots as shown in the figure.

The analysis was refined by Exner by using the equation of motion with water surface slope term and friction term. Thus a method was developed to predict modification of undulation on the bed, with the passage of time. However, this really did not fully explain formation of ripples and dunes because it did not explain how in the first place an undulation was formed on the bed. However, the importance of Exner's contribution lies in the fact that he first introduced continuity equation for sediment in the differential form.

CONCLUDING REMARKS

The major contributions in the first quarter of 20th century were relatively few. Gilbert's extensive experimentation provided a valuable data base which was subsequently used to study, bed forms, resistance and sediment transport.

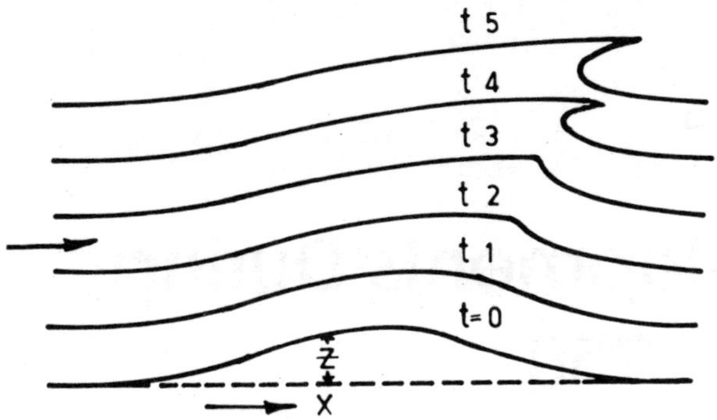

Successive modification of symmetrical undulation

Stricker's equation for resistance of plane bed was proposed. Using continuity equation for sediment, Exner showed that a small sinusoidal disturbance on the bed would develop into an unsymmetrical bed form. Lastly some minor contributions were made in regime theory of channels.

Chapter 6

Developments During 1925-1950

In general considerable progress was made in the understanding of various phases of Fluvial Hydraulics during this period. There were efforts to collect data in the laboratories; field data were collected and efforts were made to make rational analyses of the problems based on the use of dimensionless parameters and available concepts from fluid mechanics.

INCIPIENT MOTION

It was in general accepted that shear should be used as a more appropriate parameter in incipient motion studies than the average velocity. Laboratory experiments were conducted by several investigators and the critical shear τ_{oc} was related to the characteristic size d, difference in specific weights of sediment and fluid $(\gamma_s - \gamma_f)$, and some coefficient to take into account the non-uniformity of sediment, if it is so. Many of these equations could be written either as

$$\tau_{oc} / (\gamma_s - \gamma_f)\, d = \text{const., or } \tau_{oc} / (\gamma_s - \gamma_f)\, d = f(d, \text{ nonuniformity coefficient}).$$

The formulae of Krey (145) 1925, Kramer (42) 1934, Indri (145) fall under this category. A major breakthrough was made in obtaining rational solution to incipient motion condition by an American engineer A. Shields (252) 1936.

Albert Frank Shields (1908-1974), was a native Ohioan who graduated from the Stevens Institute of Technology and went to Berlin in 1933 on an exchange scholarship. He conducted an original bed-load study at the Prussian Experiment Station for Hydraulic and Marine Engineering. Applying the fluid mechanics concepts of drag and velocity distributiuon in a turbulent flow near smooth and rough surfaces and making use of dimensional reasoning, he showed that the dimensionless critical shear for uniform material should be a function of critical shear velocity Reynolds number $u_{*c}\, d\, \rho_f / \mu$ where $u_{*c} = \sqrt{\tau_{oc} / \rho_f}$ and $\mu / \rho_f = \nu$ is the kinematic viscosity. The actual relation between the two parameters $\tau_{oc} / (\gamma_s - \gamma_f)\, d$ and $u_{*c}\, d / \nu$ was determined using uniform sediments of different sizes and relative densities ranging from 1.06 to 4.25. After return to U.S.A. Shields switched to paper manufacturing business, where he had previously done some design work and in which he obtained several patents. The original paper of Shields was published in Germany in German language and the credit for getting it translated into English and making it available to the profession goes to Prof. H. Rouse. It was most unfortunate that Shields never worked again in the field of Fluvial Hydraulics, because he could have made significant contributions to other aspects of Fluvial Hydraulics. Shields died in 1974.

Further analysis of incipient motion condition was carried out by Prof. Cedric Masey White (1898 - 1993), who was Professor of Fluid Mechanics and Hydraulic Engineering in Imperial College London, upto 1966. White worked on a variety of problems in fluid mechanics and Fluvial Hydraulics such as incipient motion, secondary circulation, flow in bends, channel geometry, pipe resistance, and bed-load. Considering the case of a single particle resting on other particles, he (287) considered two cases: high speed case and low speed case. He showed that in high speed case

$$(u_{*c}\, d/\nu > 3.50) \text{ and } \tau_{oc}/(\gamma_s - \gamma_f)\, d = \frac{\pi}{6}\eta \tan\phi,$$

and in the case of low speed case

$$(u_{*c}\, d/\nu < 3.50) \text{ and } \tau_{oc}/(\gamma_s - \gamma_f)\, d = \frac{\pi}{6}\eta\alpha \tan\phi.$$

Here ϕ is angle of repose, η is the packing coefficient, $\eta = Nd^2$ (where N is number of particles per unit area), α is a coefficient which takes into account the fact that at low Reynolds number viscous force would predominate and hence force on the particle would pass through a point above the centre of gravity of particle. Values of $\alpha\eta$ were determined from experiments. In 1948 Kurihara, in Japan, analysed the problem by introducing turbulence factor T_f which was shown to be function of $u_{*c}\, d/\nu$, turbulence intensity and probability p of shear stress increment. Around the same time Tison also introduced a turbulence factor in critical tractive force analysis.

VELOCITY DISTRIBUTION AND RESISTANCE

It was during this period that the concepts of boundary layer development enunciated by Prandtl and further developed by Karman, were made available to the civil engineers through fluid mechanics texts (227, 236). As a result the velocity distribution laws in turbulent flow in pipes with hydrodynamically smooth and rough surfaces were established using Nikuradse's data. These equations, known as Karman-Prandtl's equations are

Hydrodynamically smooth boundaries

$$u/u_* = 5.75 \log(u_* y/\nu) + 5.5 \qquad (37)$$

Hydrodynamically rough boundaries

$$u/u_* = 5.75 \log(y/K_s) + 8.5$$

where K_s is the equivalent sand grain roughness. Keulegan (146) 1938, integrated the above equations over the depth of flow and obtained the following equations for average velocity U for flow in open channels. The constants in these equations were determined using Bazin's data.

$$\left.\begin{aligned}&\text{Smooth surface}\\&\qquad U/u_* = 5.75 \log (u_* R/\nu) + 3.25\\&\text{Rough surface}\\&\qquad U/u_* = 5.75 \log (R/K_s) + 6.25\end{aligned}\right\} \tag{38}$$

It can be seen that U/u_* is dimensionless Chezy's coefficient and hence Keulegan showed that for a channel $\frac{C}{\sqrt{g}}$ or $\frac{R^{1/6}}{n\sqrt{g}}$ is not constant. In general, it is a function of Reynolds number and R/K_s. For hydrodynamically smooth channels it is a function of Reynolds number. For rough channels it is a function of R/K_s, and for a boundary in transiton it depends on R/K_s and UR/ν. Some manipulation of the equation for rough boundary and its plotting as $R^{1/6}/n\sqrt{g}$ vs. R/K_s indicates that Stricker's empirical equation for $n_s = K_s^{1/6}/21$ is valid for hydrodynamically rough surfaces with R/K_s values between 7.5 and 250.

Relatively little progress was made in analysis of available data of Gilbert or those collected by United States Waterways Experiment Station to obtain resistance relationship which is valid when bed has dunes on it or when the bed forms are changing. However, the credit goes to Einstein for introducing the concept of division of total resistance to flow into grain resistance and form resistance due to dunes, which was then used to obtain a resistance predictor.

Hans Albert Einstein
(1904–1973)

Hans Albert Einstein (1904-1973), son of the famous physicist and Nobel laureate Albert Einstein, was born in 1904 in Bern, Switzerland (70, 249). He obtained his Civil Engineering degree in 1926 from the Swiss Federal Institute of Technology in Zurich, Switzerland. He then worked for few years in Ruhr valley as structural engineer and then joined the Swiss Federal Institute, Zurich in 1931 as an assistant to Meyer-Peter, who later developed Meyer Peter-Müller formula for bed-load transport. Between 1931-1938 he worked on and submitted his doctoral thesis on "Bed-load Transport as a Probabilistic Problem". In 1938 he migrated to the USA and worked as research engineer for US Dept. of Agriculture between 1938-1943. In 1947, he joined the faculty of the University of California, Berkeley (USA) and was professor there when he retired in 1971. He died in 1973. Einstein showed keen interest in nature and loved art and music; he used to play piano well. Einstein was a dedicated teacher and researcher, and an excellent lecturer and was loved by his students with whom he developed a personal relationship. He travelled widely to Asia, South America and Europe and had an intimate knowledge of the sediment problems there. Several of Einstein's doctoral candidates are presently active in reserch in Fluvial Hydraulics.

From the analysis of laboratory flume data with enhanced bank resistance, Einstein (61) in 1942 suggested a method of computing hydraulic radius with respect to bed and thus eliminate the effect of bank friction. The method involves subdivision of flow area A into area corresponding to the bed A_b and area corresponding to walls A_w. Assuming velocity to be uniform over the section, Manning's equation with known wall roughness n_w can give hydraulic radius with respect to walls as $R_w = [Un_w \mid S^{1/2}]^{3/2}$. Then knowing the perimeter with respect to the bed and to the walls, A_b and R_b can be computed. This method is very commonly used to eliminate the wall effect on the flow parameters. Further, Einstein and Banks (63), and Einstein and Barbarossa (65) proposed division of total resistance of a duned bed into the resistance offered by grains and form resistance due to dunes, and then proposed division of R_b into R'_b the hydraulic radius with respect to grains and R''_b that corresponding to form roughness. Thus bed shear τ_b will be

$$\tau_b = \tau'_b + \tau''_b$$

A major step in the analysis of resistance to flow in alluvial rivers was taken by Einstein and Barbarossa (65). Following the concept of division of R_b into R'_b and R''_b, they computed $\tau''_b = \gamma_f R''_b S$ for each set of observations by subtracting τ'_b from τ_b. In this, τ'_b was computed by using Keulegan type or Strickler type equation for grain resistance In all his analysis of sediment transport (see below), Einstein assumed that it is the shear with respect to grains τ'_b which is responsible for transport of bed-load, and hence formation of dunes. Hence, he related $\frac{U}{u''_*}$ with $\psi = \frac{(\gamma_s - \gamma_f)\, d_{35}}{\tau'_b}$ and obtained a unique curve for data from natural streams. This curve provided a means of determining average flow velocity in a stream or channel for known depth, slope, channel width, bank roughness, and sediment size distribution of the bed material. Even though questions have been raised about the uniqueness of curve, Einstein is credited for giving a logical approach to flow resistance. Later similar methods were developed by Engelund and Hansen (74, 75), and Alam and Kennedy (3).

Is it possible to predict what type of bed form would occur in a river under given flow conditions? Will the bed be rippled, duned or flat, or will it have antidunes? Gilbert (107) found that slope and the capacity *UR* play an important role in determining regimes. By plotting *UR* vs. slope, regions could be designated in which dunes, transition or antidunes would form. Forchheimer (111) 1930 indicated that Froude number $U/\sqrt{gR}$ serves as a useful criterion for prediction of regimes; if Fr is less than unity, bed will have dunes; if Fr is greater than unity, antidunes will form. On Shields' diagram of $\tau_o/(\gamma_s - \gamma_f)\,d$ vs. $u_*\,d/\nu$ regions were shown in which different bed forms would occur.

Walter Basil Langbein (1907-) was born at Newark (N.J.), USA in 1907 and has worked with the US Geological Survey since 1935; he has contributed significantly in the field of hydrology. In 1942, Langbein (178) used Gilbert's data and by plotting $U/\sqrt{gR}$ vs. *UR* he obtained criterion for regime prediction for a given sediment size.Thus it can be said that by this time it was realised that Froude number should play an important role in the prediction of regimes. However, no generalised criteron was available.

BED-LOAD TRANSPORT

During this period several engineers in USA conducted experiments on bed-load transport. Flume experiments were carried out by MacDougall at M I.T. in 1933, by Mavis *et al.* (196, 197) at the University of Iowa during 1935-37, Waterways Experiment Station at Vicksburg in 1935, by Obrien and his co-workers at the University of California, Berkeley in 1935, and by Chang in 1939. Similar experiments were conducted in Europe by Donat in 1929, Shields in 1936 and Schoklitsch. In the former USSR Velikanov, Bochkov, Goncharov, Shamov, Pushkarev conducted experiments on bed undulations and bed-load transport. These studies resulted in empirical bed-load equations which can be written in one of the following forms.

$q_B = f(q - q_c)$	McDougall, Straub, Schoklitsch
$q_B = f(\tau_o - \tau_{oc})$	Obrien & Rindlaub, USWES, Chang, Chyn
$q_B = f(U - U_c)$	Nakayama, Goncharov, Shamov

where q, τ_o, U are the unit discharge, bed shear and average velocity of flow and q_c, τ_{oc}, and U_c are the critical values at which the sediment starts moving. Most of these equations were based on laboratary experiments using uniform or nearly uniform materials. Also, many of them used Gilbert's data. Being empirical in nature these equations were unlikely to give reliable estimates of bed-load in natural streams. Schoklitsch after analysis of bed-load data of sediment mixtures recommended that a size between d_{40} and d_{60} can be used as the representative size.

The most commonly used and fairly accurate empirical bed-load equation was developed by Meyer Peter and Müller of the Swiss Federal Institute of Technology.

Eugene Meyer-Peter
(1883-1969)

Robert Müller
(1908-1987)

Eugen Meyer Peter (1883-1969), was born in 1883 in Kewrisau (Appenzell) and studied in ETH, Zurich from 1901-1905. After gaining experience in the construction of docks and harbours and power plant projects of Argestwyhlen, Albula and Felsenan for about 14 years, he was invited to ETH to be a teacher. Here he worked for 33 years as teacher, research worker and an expert of international standing. On his initiative Hydraulics Laboratory was built in ETH in 1930 which was headed by him. Meyer Peter retired from the teaching job in 1952 and from the directorship of Institute of Hydraulics and Soil Mechanics in 1953. He died in Zurich in 1969.

His colleague Robert Müller (1908-1987) was born in Baden, Switzerland in 1908 and was educated in ETH Zurich. In 1931, he was appointed as assistant to Prof. Meyer Peter. After Henry Favre he was appointed as head of Hydraulics Department in 1938. Hans Albert Einstein was working here at that time, who migrated to the USA in 1938. Favre, Einstein, Müller and Meyer Peter worked on the problem of bed-load equation, which led to the development of Meyer Peter and Müller formula for bed-load. In 1957 Dr. Müller retired from ETH as professor of hydraulics and became director of the Second Correction of the Jura Waters.The work mainly consisted of river training to connect three natural lakes Murten, Neuchatel and Bienne, thus providing a large flood retention basin for the main tribuary Aare. He expired in 1987.

The main features of Meyer Peter and Müller's bed-load equation, which is essentially empirical in nature, are the following

1. It is based on a wide rage of data

Slope	S	0.0004 to 0.02
	d	0.4 mm to 30 mm

Depth D	0.01 m to 1.20 m		
Relative density	2.68,	4.22,	1.25
	Gravel	Baryta	Lignite

2. It uses grain shear as parameter responsible for bed-load transport. It was obtained by dividing slope S into S' and S'', slope required to overcome grain resistance and form resistance respectively.
3. As long as all the particles are moving use of average size of material d_a is adequate.

Earlier Meyer Peter, Favre and Einstein had suggested a bed-load equation which was modified by Meyer Peter and Müller. The resulting equation is

$$\left(\frac{n_s}{n}\right)^{3/2} \frac{\gamma_f R_b S}{(\gamma_s - \gamma_f)\, d_a} = 0.047 + 0.25 \left(\frac{\gamma_f}{g}\right)^{1/3} \left(\frac{q_B}{\gamma_s}\right) \frac{1}{(\gamma_s - \gamma_f)^{1/3}\, d_a} \tag{39}$$

which has been put in the following alternate forms by Ning Chien (209).

$$\left.\begin{aligned} &\left(\frac{n_s}{n}\right)^{3/2} \tau_* = 0.047 + 0.25\, \phi_B^{2/3} \\ \text{or}\quad & 8\,(\tau_*' - 0.047)^{3/2} = \phi_B \\ \text{where}\quad & \tau_*' = \gamma_f R_b' S / (\gamma_s - \gamma_f)\, d_a,\ \ \phi_B = \frac{q_B}{\gamma_s} \sqrt{\frac{\rho_f}{\rho_s - \rho_f}} \left(\frac{1}{g d_a^3}\right)^{1/2} \end{aligned}\right\} \tag{40}$$

Ning Chien (209) has shown that the above equation predicts the bed-load rate as satisfactory as Einstein's bed-load equation (see below) for uniform sediment and also for non-uniform sediment if only a single characteristic size is used in Einstein's bed-load equation.

Two bed-load equations, that were developed during this period and which are more analytical in nature than Meyer Peter, Müller's equation, are those of Einstein and Kalinske.

The credit goes to Einstein for developing a semi-theoretical equation for bed-load transport (61). This was later modified and a detailed procedure was given by him for computation of bed-load, suspended load and the total load. His equation is based on the following premises: (i) Sediment movement is probabilistic in nature and hence there is nothing like a critical tractive stress. Even at very low shear value there will be occasional movement of a particle. (ii) When the instantaneous lift on a particle exceeds its submerged weight, the particle is dislodged. (iii) Once the particle is in motion, the probability of it being redeposited is assumed to be equal at all the points where the local flow would not dislodge the particle again immediately. (iv) Average distance travelled by any particle moving as bed-load between consecutive points of deposition is assumed to be constant and this is independent of the flow conditions, transport rate and bed composition.

The different transport rates are then achieved by a change in the average time between two steps. In his publication (64) of 1950, Einstein related bed-load to suspended load of a given size fraction by arguing that average concentration of bed-load in a layer of $2d$ thickness is equal to the concentration of suspended load there. This was a very ingeneous way to relate suspended load to bed-load transport, and this was necessary since suspended load transport is an advanced stage of bed-load transport. Einstein and Barbarossa's resistance method and Einstein's method of calculation of sediment load have been the subject of further verification and modification by many investigators. Certain discrepancies have been pointed out. However, it is agreed by the most that in spite of these limitations, Einstein's contributions to Fluvial Hydraulics have been the most important.

Einstein also deserves credit for formalising the concept of wash load. Even though Vetter (281) 1937, was probably the first one to recognise the need for division of suspended load into two parts, viz. that composed of those sizes which are found in abundance in the bed material, and that composed of those fine sizes which are not available in appreciable quantities in the bed. Einstein et al. (61) 1942, first suggested the division of total load into bed material load and the wash load. Since wash load is brought into the stream from the drainage area upstream, its amount is not related to the hydraulic conditions of the stream at that section, but is related to its availability in the drainage basin and the hydrologic characteristics there. Later Einstein (64) recommended that the limiting size for the wash load may be arbitrarily chosen from the mechanical analysis of the bed material, as that particle size for which ten per cent of the bed material is finer than this size.

Anthonie Adam Kalinske
(1911–)

Anthonie Adam Kalinske (1911-) was born in 1911 in Wisconsin, USA and educated there. Then he joined Iowa Institute of Hydraulic Research in the latter part of thirties. His research interests included turbulence, diffusion and sediment transport. To a great extent he was responsible for initiating Naval research in Iowa during the second World War. He is also given some credit for conducting wind tunnel and water tunnel studies at Iowa.

Kalinske was working at Iowa as contemporary of late Prof. E. W. Lane. Various aspects of sediment transport such as saltation (152), bed-load, and calculation of suspended load were studied by them. He showed that for the same conditions of shear stress on the bed and particle size, the height of saltation would depend on the density ratio between sediment and fluid. Hence saltation in air will be about 800 times that in water for a sand particle. Kalinske developed (153) a bed-load equation which took into account the turbulent velocity fluctuations near the boundary and hence the shear stress on the bed. Turbulent velocity fluctuations were assumed to be normally distributed. Bed-load equation was developed for uniform material; however for non-uniform sediments the bed-load rate can be computed from the relation $q_B = \Sigma\, q_{Bi}\, \Delta p_i$ where Δp_i is fraction of the bed-material of size d_i in the bed. Kalinske later switched over to environmental engineering consultancy.

It would be appropriate to mention here briefly about the contributions of William Walden Rubey from USA. Rubey (1898 -1974) was born in Moberly (Mo), USA in 1898 and received his graduate degree from Missouri. He worked from 1920 to 1960 with the U.S. Geological Survey in various capacities. In between, he was also professor of geology and geophysics in the University of California, Los Angeles and visiting professor at California Institute of Technology. He died in 1974. Rubey suggested (240) 1933, a formula for fall velocity of coarse materials outside Stokes' range. Equating submerged weight of particle to the summation of viscous resistance and impact resistance, he obtained the equation

$$\omega_0 = \sqrt{\frac{36\mu^2}{\rho_f^2\, d^2} + \frac{2}{3}\frac{(\gamma_s - \gamma_f)d}{\rho_f}} - \frac{6\mu}{\rho_f\, d} \tag{41}$$

This equation gives good results only upto $\omega_0\, d\, \rho_f / \mu = 10$. In another paper Rubey (242) 1938, used the concept of energy balance in sediment laden streams and showed that average sediment concentration in a stream $\overline{C}_s$ is proportional to $R^{1/2}\, S^{2/3}$. Since unit discharge $q \sim R^{3/2}\, S^{1/2}$

$$q_s = q\,\overline{C}_s \sim R^2\, S^{7/6}$$

This concept of energy balance was later used by Bagnold and Velikanov. Rubey (242) 1938, analysed the incipient motion condition using average critical velocity and he found that particle weight W and U_c are related $U_c^6 \sim W$. He also independently recommended use of d / δ' in the critical motion studies. Here δ' is the thickness of laminar sublayer.

SUSPENDED SEDIMENT TRANSPORT

As mentioned earlier, prior to 1925, many investigators had put forward several qualitativte ideas about suspension of sediment. Dupuit (59) 1865, believed that suspension was caused by the differences in the magnitudes of velocities of the adjacent fluid particles, i.e. it is dependent on the velocity gradient. He also mentioned that agent opposing the suspension is the settling velcoity of solid particles. Partiot (224) and Lechalas (182) in 1871, and Kennedy (158) 1895, assumed that turbulent eddies are responsible for suspension ahd these eddies near the bed throw the material on the bed in suspension. Krey (167) 1925, proposed that the upward velocity component of turbulent velocity is proportional to the Reynolds number UD/ν and a power law type relationship can be obtained between turbulent velocity component and the Reynolds number. It was also observed by several investigators, such as Forshey in 1851, Surell on the Rhone, and Buckley (36) 1922, that the suspended sediment concentration is higher near the bottom and smaller near the surface. A significant impetus to the analysis of suspension of sediment was given by the German meteorologist Schmidt (as given in 215) 1925, who while studying the distribution of dust in the atmosphere, wrote the differential equation

$$\omega_0 C + \varepsilon_s \frac{\partial C}{\partial y} = 0 \qquad (42)$$

where C is the concentration of suspended sediment at a distance y from the bed, ω_0 is the fall velocity of sediment and ε_s is the sediment transfer coefficient. He gave ε_s as a function of y. This equation was also obtained by Obrien (as mentioned in 215) 1933, by equating the upward transfer of sediment with the settling rate of sediment.

In a discussion on Obrien's paper, Karman suggested that momentum transfer cefficient ε_m is related to velocity gradient and one can assume $\varepsilon_s = \varepsilon_m$ and integrate the above equation. Hurst (135) 1929, and Rouse (237) 1938 independently conducted experiments in laboratory in containers in which artificial turbulence was created either by rotation of paddles or by oscillations of a grid. Both verified the above equation in its integrated form using constant ε_s.

Integration of Eq. 42 needs knowledge about variation of ε_s with y. This was provided by the works of Karman and Prandtl on velocity distribution in turbulent flow near hydrodynamically smooth and rough surfaces.

Theodor Von Karman (1881–1963)

Theodor Von Karman, who was the son of the professor at the university of Budapest, was born at Budapest in 1881. After graduating in mechanical engineering from the Royal Polytechnic Institute in Budapest, Karman worked under Ludwig Prandtl and obtained the doctorate from the University of Göttingen . He started his teaching career in the same institute. In 1913 he was made the director of the newly established aeronautical laboratory at the Polytechnic Institute of Aachen (Germany). He moved to the California Institute of Technology, Pasadena (USA) in 1927 and was made the director of Guggenheim Aeronautical Laboratory in the same institute in 1930. He expired in 1963 in Aachen.

Due to his deep insight in the problems on which he worked and his mastery over the mathematical techniques, during his active life, Karman worked and excelled in different fields of mechanics and made very significant contributions. In the field of fluid mechanics Karman's contributions concerning stability of alternate vortices behind two-dimensional bodies (known as Karman vortex trail), computation of two-dimensional boundary layers on flat plate with pressure gradient using momentum equation, various aspects of statistical theory of turbulence, use of similarity hypothesis in phenomenological theories of turbulence, Karman-Prandtl equations for velocity distribution in turbulent flow near hydrodynamically smooth and rough surfaces, skin friction on flat plates, and resistance to flow in pipes, are well known. In the field of Fluvial Hydraulics, the velocity distribution laws that he and Prandtl developed and which were modified by Keulegan form the basis of further work on the subject. Further, for some period when H. Rouse and A.T. Ippen were at the California Institute of Technology, it seems that Karman directly or indirectly influenced the work they did on sediment suspension. Lastly, in 1947 he wrote a paper (155) in which he tried to explain the formation of ripples in the desert. The constancy or otherwise of the Karman constant in sediment laden flows with and without bed undulations has created considerable debate and research activity during the past half century.

Rouse and Ippen were both working at the California Institute of Technology, USA during 1930s. Rouse was working for Soil Conservation Service. At the suggestion of Karman, who was working in CALTEC at that time, Rouse obtained integration of Eq.42 by using $\varepsilon_s = \varepsilon_m$ and obtaining the latter as $\varepsilon_m = u_* \kappa y (D-y)/D$ from velocity distribution law. Here u_* is the shear velocity $\sqrt{\tau_0/\rho_f}$, τ_0 is the shear stress on the bed, and κ is Karman constant = 0.40. This resulted in the sediment distribution equation as

$$\left.\begin{aligned} C/C_a &= \left(\frac{D-y}{y}\,\frac{a}{D-a}\right)^{Z} \\ Z &= \omega_0/u_*\,\kappa \end{aligned}\right\} \quad (43)$$

Here C_a is concentration of sediment at distance a from bed. This equation is often known as Rouse equation. Ippen integrated Eq. (42) using Krey's equation for velocity distribution in place of Karman-Prandtl equation and hence the resulting equation had a different form. Whereas Rouse equation gives zero concentration at water surface and infinite concentration at the bed, Ippen's equation gave zero concentration at the water surface and finite concentration at the bed. Hayami (121) 1938 also obtained Eq. (42) after simplifying the general diffusion equation and assuming $\varepsilon_s = \varepsilon_m$; however, he evaluated ε_m in a somewhat different manner.

Arthur Thomas Ippen (1907-1974) was born in July 1907 in London, UK, of German parents. He had his secondary and higher education in Aachen and obtained Diploma Ingenieur in Civil Engineering from the Technische Hochschule in 1931. In 1932 he came to USA and studied at the State University of Iowa and California Institute of Technology under Professor R.T. Knapp and Theodor Von Karman. He worked on sediment suspension and high velocity flows. After

Arthur Thomas Ippen
(1907–1974)

Vito A. Vanoni
(1904–)

receiving Ph.D. from CALTEC, Ippen worked from 1938 to 1945 at Lehigh University in Bethelhem (Pennsylvania), USA and then moved to Massachusetts Institute of Technology in 1945 as Associate Professor. He worked in M.I.T. till June 1973 when he retired to become Professor Emeritus. During this period he was responsible for revitalising research in Hydraulics and Hydrodynamics in the area of liquid, free surface and solid-liquid systems. He also worked in the areas of coastal and estuarine problems. He expired in April 1974 at the age of 66. In the area of Fluvial Hydraulics, Ippen contributed to the development of equation for distribution of suspended load in channels, variation of Karman constant in the presence of suspended sediment, distribution of shear stress in bends, and velocity distribution and stability of underflows.

Verification of Eq. 43 in laboratory channels and streams was carried out by many investigators. Among them mention may be made of Vanoni and Anderson.

Vito A.Vanoni (1904-) was born in Samis, California (USA) in 1904. He had his engineering education (B.S., M.S. and Ph.D.) from the California Institute of Technology, Pasadena (California), USA, where he also started his teaching career in 1942 as assistant Professor and rose to the level of Professor in 1955. Since 1974 he is Professor Emeritus at the same place. In 1946 he reported (276) detailed experiments conducted by him to verify sediment distribution Eq. (43). Verification in the field was carried out by Anderson (7). Later under Vanoni's guidance investigations on various aspects of Fluvial Hydraulics were carried out by Hsu, N.H. Brooks, G.N. Nomicos, J.F. Kennedy, L.S. Hwang, and B.D. Taylor. These aspects include effects of suspended load on flow characteristics, resistance and suspended load, antidune formation, effect of temperature, and form roughness. Later Vanoni was also responsible for editing a Sedimentation Manual of ASCE, which summarised the then state of knowledge on the subject.

The verification of suspended load distribution equation using laboratory data and field data raised certain questions. These were (i) why does the observed Z value in Eq. (43) not agree with the computed value? (ii) Does the value of Karman constant remain at about 0.40 – the clear water value or is it affected by suspended sediment and bed undulations? (iii) How is the reference concentration C_a in Eq. (43) to be predicted? The first two questions were investigated later whereas solution to the third was provided by Lane and Kalinske, and Einstein.

Emory Wilson Lane
(1891-1963)

Emory Wilson Lane (1891-1963) studied at Purdue and Cornell and then had considerable experience both in USA and in China with Morgan Engineering Company and various Federal Bureaus in USA. He moved to the Iowa Institute of Hydraulic Research in 1935 and then temporarily moved to Tennessee Valley Authority in 1942. He later returned to Iowa. Later Lane also worked for Bureau of Reclamation and as Professor in Colorado State University, Fort Collins, USA. He expired in 1963. Lane and Kalinske (173) 1939 obtained a relation between (suspended sediment concentration near bed/fraction of that sized material in bed) and u_* / ω_0. They also proposed a method (174) 1941, for quick calculation of suspended sediment load based on the integration of *Cu* curves. Earlier, Lane (172) 1937, had shown that Lacey's method of channel design is not applicable to canals in other countries indicating that sediment load is an important factor in channel design which is ignored in Lacey's method. Lane has also published papers on density of deposited sediment in reservoirs, reservoir sedimentation, cutoffs and river morphology. Even though some of this work is qualitative in nature it shows Lane's understanding of complex river behaviour and his pragmatic approach to the advancement of knowledge based on field observations. Along with other engineers, Lane was also associated with the production of ten reports by Miami Conservancy District, on Miami Flood Control Project, Hydraulic Jump and Backwater Curves, Hydraulic Jump as an Energy Dissipator, Calculations of Open Channel Flow, Hydraulics of the Miami Flood Control Project, etc. Further, under Prof. Lane's guidance a cooperative effort was started at Iowa on equipment and practices about sediment sampling. This is discussed later under Sediment Sampling.

It was also during this period that the diffusion equation in its complete form was considered by Dobbins (56) 1941, and applied to transient non-uniform conditions by Dobbins (56), and Kalinske (151). The general diffusion equation is

$$\frac{\partial C}{\partial t} + u\frac{\partial C}{\partial x} + v\frac{\partial C}{\partial y} + w\frac{\partial C}{\partial z} = \frac{\partial}{\partial x}\left(\varepsilon_x \frac{\partial C}{\partial x}\right) + \frac{\partial}{\partial y}\left(\varepsilon_y \frac{\partial C}{\partial y}\right) + \frac{\partial}{\partial z}\left(\varepsilon_z \frac{\partial C}{\partial z}\right) + \omega_0 \frac{\partial C}{\partial y} \tag{44}$$

Assuming two dimensional flow and $\frac{\partial^2 C}{\partial x^2} << \frac{\partial^2 C}{\partial y^2}$, the above equation was simplified to

$$\frac{\partial C}{\partial t} + u\frac{\partial C}{\partial x} = \omega_0 \frac{\partial C}{\partial y} + \varepsilon_s \frac{\partial^2 C}{\partial y^2} \tag{45}$$

When $v = w = 0$ and $\partial C / \partial t$ is very small compared to other terms, Eq. (45) becomes

$$u\frac{\partial C}{\partial x} = \omega_0 \frac{\partial C}{\partial y} + \varepsilon_s \frac{\partial^2 C}{\partial y^2} \tag{46}$$

This has been studied by Dobbins and Kalinske for different boundary conditions.

SEDIMENT SAMPLING

During the period under consideration several bed-load samplers were developed in Europe and the former USSR where bed-load transport is predominant in many streams (132). Basket type Davis sampler was developed in USA in 1898. Samplers developed by Bogardi, Nesper, Muhlhofer, Ehrenberger and the Swiss Federal Authority are also of basket type; some of these are shown in the adjoining figures. All these samplers are similar in dessign but each is an improvement over it's predecessor. Laboratory experiments were performed to determine the efficiency of these samplers. Using these samplers field data were collected and used to develop or check bed-load equations of Schoklitsch, and Meyer Peter and Müller. Pan type samplers were developed primarily in the former USSR. Two such samplers named after Losiebsky and Polyakov are shown in the figure. Shamov studied the efficiency of Losiebsky, Polykaov and SRIH (Scientific Research Institute of Hydrotechnics) samplers which was found to be 38, 46 and 75 per cent respectively. Pressure difference type samplers were fabricated by Goncharov in USSR and by J.M. Terry of the US Geological Survey in USA. Arnhem and VUV samplers are shown in the figure. In USA Einstein measured the bed-load of the Enoree river and the Mountain Creek using pit type sampler in which continuous withdrawal of bed-load was effected and its weighing arranged. A recently developed pit type sampler is also shown in the figure.

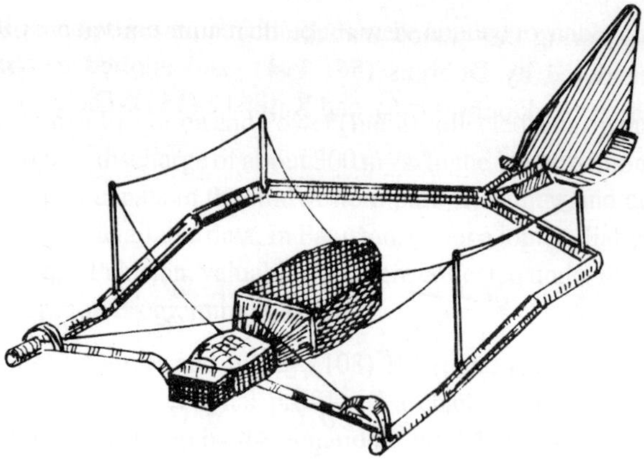

Arnhem sampler (1935)

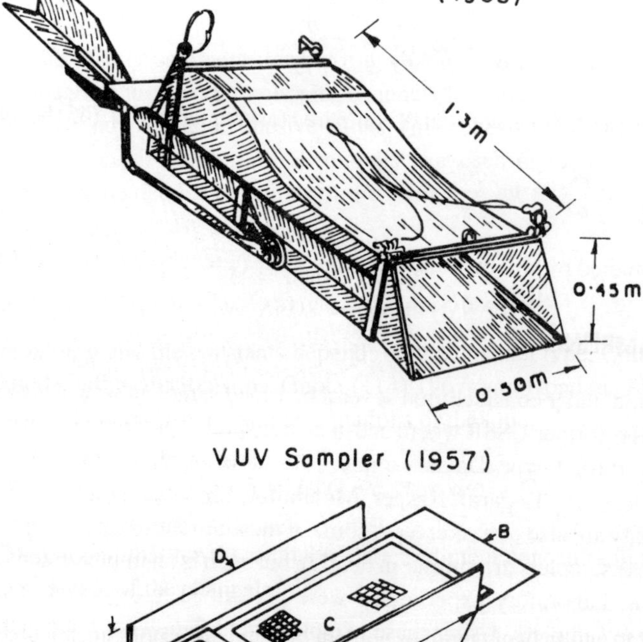

VUV Sampler (1957)

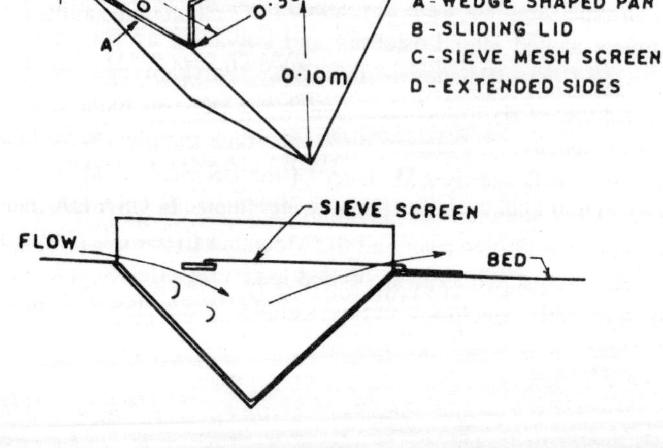

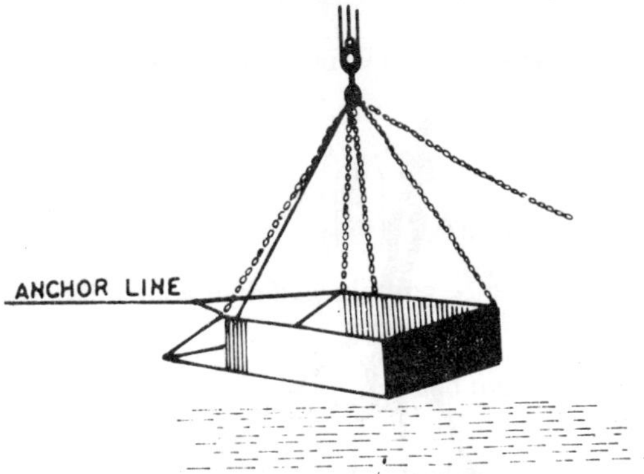

Davis sampler (1898)

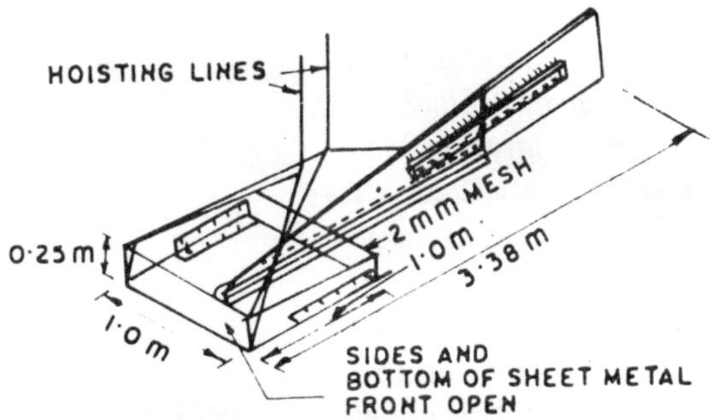

Bogardi sampler (1936)

Nesper bed-load sampler (1937)

Some bed-load samplers

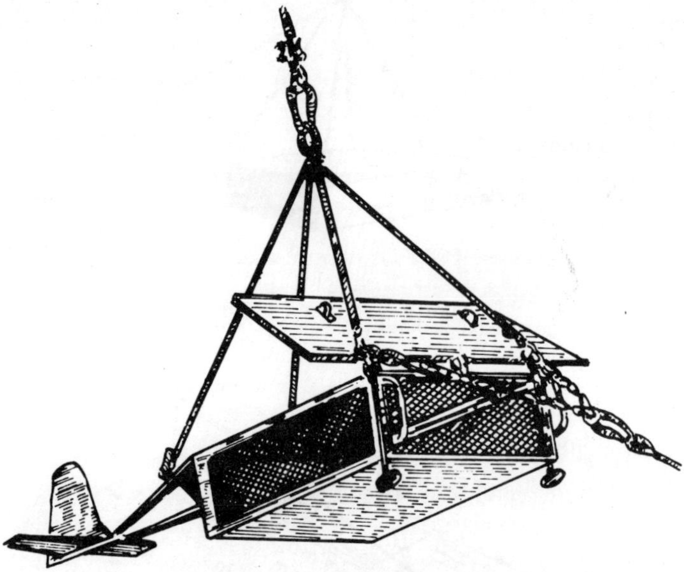

Mühlhofer sampler (1932)

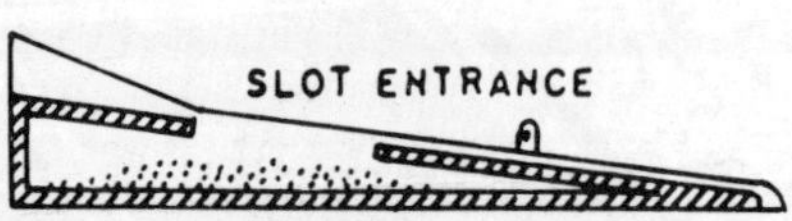

Losiebsky pan sampler (1935)

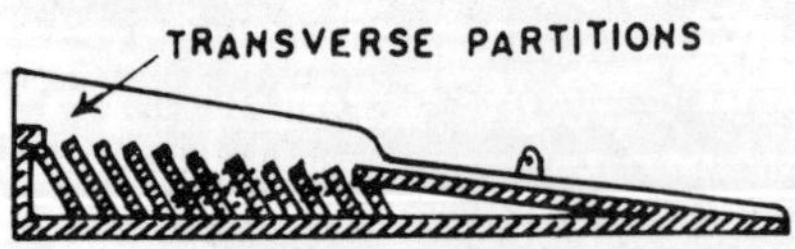

Polyakov pan sampler (1935)

Some bed-load samplers

In the USA a comprehensive programme was initiated in 1939 through an interdepartmental sedimentation committee involving the Geological Survey, Indian Service, the Bureau of Reclamation of the U.S. Department of Interior, the Flood Control Coordination Committee of the US Department of Agriculture, the US Engineers of the War Department, and Tennessee Valley Authority. The investigation was conducted at the Hydraulic Laboratory of Iowa Institute of Hydraulic Research, State University of Iowa under the supervision of Late Prof. E.W. Lane. The Headquarters of the committee was shifted to Saint Anthony falls Laboratory at Minneapolis in 1948. The committee produced the following reports.

Rep. No. 1. Field Practice and Equipment Used in Sampling Suspended Sediment.

2. Equipment Used for Sampling Bed-Load and Bed-Material.
3. Analytical Study of Methods of Sampling Suspended Sediment.
4. Methods of Analysing Sediment Samples.
5. Laboratory Investigations of Suspended Sediment Samplers.
6. Design of Improved Types of Suspended Sediment Samplers.
7. A Study of New Methods of Size Analysis of Suspended Sediment Samplers.
8. Measurement of Sediment Discharge of Streams.
9. Density of Sediments Deposited in Reservoirs.
10. Accuracy of Sediment Size Analysis Made by the Bottom Withdrawal — Tube Method.

In these reports a wealth of information is available on sampling, and the related aspects. These reports collate information available at that time in different countries and try to recommend methods. Under this project new equipments were also developed and tested later on.

It is interesting to note how the sampling procedures for suspended sediment were gradually evolved. In the earlier stages of development equal weightage was given to the samples collected at different depths.The more rational method of giving twice the weight to the midsample seems to be a relatively recent development, the first record found being that of U.S. Engineering Department, sampling in the Mississippi in 1930. In 1931, Forshey used the surface samples at Carrollton in the Mississippi river and applied a coefficient of 1.2 to get the average sediment concentration. The practice of taking samples at 0.60 depth without applying any correction has been the common practice since 1912 when it was apparently first used in rivers in Turkey. A rational analysis for determining the position and weightages of sampling points in the vertical seems to have been derived to have methods applicable to linear and non-linear distributions of suspended sediment. In the former case observations were made and 0.20 and 0.80 depth with weights of 5 and 3 applied as recommended by Straub. Since Straub's analysis is not found is most of the texts, it is briefly summarised below:

The velocity distribution in the Missouri river in USA could be expressed by the power law,

$$u / u_s = (y / D)^m = \eta^m \tag{47}$$

where u is the velocity at distance y above the bed, u_s is the velocity at the surface, D is the depth of flow, m is a constant and η is dimenstionless vertical distance. The exponent m was found to be 0.284. Hence discharge per unit width q is given by

$$\left.\begin{aligned} q &= \int_0^D u dy = u_s D \int_0^1 \eta^m d\eta \\ \text{or} \quad q &= \frac{u_s D}{(m+1)} \end{aligned}\right\} \tag{48}$$

For most of the Missouri river stations at which samples were taken, the concentration distribution was found to be linear, viz.

$$C = C_0 - \eta (C_0 - C_s) \tag{49}$$

where C_o and C_s are concentrations at the bed and surface respectively and C is concentration at any distance y above the bed. Hence suspended load carried per unit width per second, q_s

$$q_s = \int_0^D uC\, dy = u_s D \int_0^1 \eta^m (C_o - \eta (C_o - C_s))\, d\eta$$

$$\text{or} \quad q_s = \frac{u_s D [C_o + (m+1) C_s]}{(m+1)(m+2)} \tag{50}$$

Substituting $u_s D = q (m+1)$ and $\overline{C}_s = q_s / q$ one gets

$$\overline{C}_s = \frac{[C_o + (m+1) C_s]}{(m+2)} = \kappa_1 C_0 + \kappa_2 C_s \tag{51}$$

Further, for linear variation of concentration, $C_{0.20D}$ and $C_{0.80D}$ depend on C_o and C_s, and hence in Eq. (51) C_o and C_s can be replaced by $C_{0.20D}$ and $C_{0.80D}$ with different coefficients. Hence $\overline{C}_s$ can be expressed as

$$\overline{C}_s = K_1 C_{0.20D} + K_2 C_{0.80D} \tag{52}$$

Where K_1 and K_2 would depend on the exponent m.

Since 1935 onwards a better understanding of the velocity distribution and the distribution of suspended sediment was gained because of the contributions of Keulegan, Karman, Rouse and Ippen. Simultaneously there was greater awareness among the engineers about need for systematic and regular collection of suspended sediment data. These led to the rapid progress in development of suspended sediment samplers and in the sampling techniques as regards the frequency, location of verticals and location of the sampling points in the vertical. Planned programme in the USA by the US Geological Survey has been responsible for the developments in the measuring equipment and procedures in the past four decades.

In India suspended sediment sampling was done by bottle type samplers known as Punjab Bottle Sampler in which a closed bottle is lowered to a desired depth and then opened and closed so that it gets filled. Such a sampler is known to be hydraulically defective and is found to underestimate the suspended sediment concentration for the medium and coarse sediments. However, in spite of this defect it continues to be used because of its simplicity and cost effectiveness. Bottle type sampler was earlier developed and used in USA at the end of 19th century. In India it was devised in 1935 by the Punjab Irrigation Department. Some modifications in the bottle type sampler were made by Framji and Raisinghani, Hoon, and Sarkar (as mentioned in 39). It may also be mentioned that the Tait Bincley sampler developed in the USA was modified by Puri and H.L. Uppal.

Between 1960 and 1970 some work was done in India on the prediction of efficiency of the bottle type sampler. These studies indicated that, at 0.6*D*, for the coarse (greater than 0.20 mm) and medium (between 0.20 mm and 0.075 mm) sized sediment the sampling efficiency ranged between 70 to 75 per cent and about 93 per cent respectively (39).

Hunter Rouse
(1906-)

Prof. Hunter Rouse (1906-) was born in Toledo, Ohio (USA) in 1906 and had his early education there (156). He joined MIT in 1926 and graduated in Civil Engineering in 1929. Immediately after graduation he left for Germany and spent a year at Karlsruhe in Germany with T. Rehbock, working on his Master's thesis project related to flow over free overfall (which he later submitted at MIT), learning French and German, and travelling through France, Italy, Germany and Switzerland to see the hydraulic laboratories and write about them. When he returned, he was appointed as Assistant in Hydraulics at MIT where he continued his work on Master's and doctoral problems. He submitted his doctoral thesis at Karlsruhe in Germany in 1932 itself. Thereafter he held various posts in American Universities viz. 1933-35 at Columbia University with Boris K. Bakhmeteff; and 1935-1939 Sedimentation Laboratory of Soil Conservation Service at CALTEC with Knapp and V.A. Vanoni. At CALTEC Ippen was also working at about the same time and both

Ippen and Rouse were influenced by Theodor Von Karman. Einstein was also there. Rouse did the work on distribution of suspended sediment at CALTEC. As mentioned earlier, Ippen also worked on it independently using a different velocity distributuion law. In 1939, Rouse moved to Iowa University and became the director of Iowa Institute of Hydraulic Reserach in 1943, after Prof. E.W. Lane left for TVA in 1942. IIHR held triennial Hydraulics Conferences starting from 1939 and the last one was held in 1958. The proceedings of 4th Conference were edited by Rouse and published in book form under the title "Engineering Hydraulics" which is an excellent book incorporating principles of Fluid Mechanics in Hydraulic Engineering. This book contained one chapter on sediment transport.

At Iowa under the direction of Rouse several problems related to cavitation, heat convection, roughness, free-turbulence shear flows, flow in open channels, turbulent diffusion, sediment transport and boundary layers were studied. Rouse wrote four books on Basic Fluid Mechanics and Advanced Fluid Mechanics which are considered to be classics. Rouse is greatly responsible for introduction and promotion of fluid mechanics in conventional hydraulic engineering problems, thereby making their analysis more rational and general. Just as Prandtl, Rouse has also emphasised the necessity of judicious combination of theoretical analysis and experimental work in solution of problems.

In the area of Fluvial Hydraulics, in addition to theoretical and experimental work on sediment suspension (237, 238) he has done work on fall velocity, application of turbulence theory to sediment transport, diffusion of jet with suspended sediment, analysis of resistance in open channels, and characteristics of flow with density stratification. Rouse relinquished the post of director of IIHR in 1966 and was dean of Engineering in Iowa University for five years. During his academic career he guided thirty five doctoral theses and many of his doctoral candidates, at present are actively involved in research in many universities and research laboratories.

It would be appropriate to mention about another American Engineer who has been responsible for advancement of Fluvial Hydraulics in U.S.A. Lorenz G. Straub (1901-1963) was trained as structural engineer but switched over to hydraulics after visiting Germany as the Freeman Scholar. He built St. Anthony Falls Laboratory at St. Paul, Minnisota (U.S.A.) and was the founder Director of that laboratory, in which capacity he worked till his death. He was also very active in IAHR activities and was a frequent consultant in hydraulics all over the world.

Straub's contributions to Fluvial Hydraulics have been varied. Using Gilbert's data he determined the value of τ_{oc} and the contant A occurring in du Boy's bed-load equation. He also developed an empirical bed-load equation in terms of q and q_c. Straub investigated the relationship between mean concentration of suspended sediment $\overline{C}_s$ and concentrations at 0.2D and 0.8D; viz.

$$\overline{C}_s = \left[\frac{3}{8} C_{0.20D} + \frac{5}{8} C_{0.8D}\right]$$

Loren G. Straub
(1901-1963)

In 1935 Straub presented a report on the Missouri river to the U.S. Govt which is often quoted. In addition, he worked on the effect of channel contraction works on the regime of an alluvial river, effect of water temperature on suspended sediment load, etc. Work on sediment problems at S.A.F. laboratory was later continued by Allen George Anderson (1911-1975). Anderson was born and educated in Minnesota. He had earlier worked with the Soil Conservation Service Sediment Laboratory at Greenville (S.C.) before joining Minnesota.

CHANNELS AND RIVERS

Stable Channels

The most significant contribution to the development of design procedure for stable or regime channels was made by Gerald Lacey (1887-1980) who was born in UK in 1887 and after his education there, he joined the Indian Service of Engineering in 1910 (205). He worked in Thomason College of Engineering, Roorkee (now University of Roorkee, U.P., India) during 1915-1917, 1928-1932 and 1945-1946 in various capacities including as professor and finally as Principal. During 1917-1919 he was in the war service and again during 1942-1944 he was Lieutenant Colonel in the Corps of Engineers posted as officer commanding in charge of technical training. Between 1924-1927 and 1933-1941 he was in the Irrigation Department of Uttar Pradesh (India), initially as Under Secretary and then as Chief Engineer. He retired in 1946 after two years tenure as Principal at Thomason College of Engineering and settled in U.K. He expired at the age of 92 in 1980.

Gerald Lacey
(1887-1980)

He analysed the then available data on stable channels from India which were flowing through sandy materials and were carrying a relatively small amount of bed material load since sediment excluders were invariably provided at the headworks and many times an ejector in the upstream reaches of the canals. In

1929 he published a paper (169) in the Proceedings of Institution of Civil Engineers, London; then in 1932 published Tech. Paper No. 1 U.P.P.W.D. and in 1936 Tech. Paper No. 20 of Central Board of Irrigation and Power (India). In these papers he presented the following equations, which were given by him in FPS units and are here converted in MKS units.

$$\left.\begin{aligned} P &= 4.75\sqrt{Q} \\ R &= 0.47\left(\frac{Q}{f_1}\right)^{1/3} \\ S &= 0.0003\, f_1^{5/3}/Q^{1/6} \\ U &= 0.516\, f_1^{5/3}\, Q^{1/6} = 10.8\, R^{2/3} S^{1/2} \\ f_1 &= 1.76\sqrt{d} \end{aligned}\right\} \tag{53}$$

Here P is the perimeter, R is the hydraulic radius, U is the average velocity, S is the channel slope, Q is the discharge, f_1 is the silt factor and d is the median size of bed material in mm. For wider rivers, equation for R in terms of unit discharge q (discharge per unit width) obtained by combining the first two equations is used viz.,

$$R = 1.35\,(q^2/f_1)^{1/3} \tag{54}$$

The equations of R (Eq. 54), S and U of Lacey are widely used in India for sandy rivers at bankful discharge. In his later publications Lacey continued to change constants in the equations and attempted to explain deviations; however, his equations quoted above are more often used in India.

Application of Lacey's equations to canals outside India has met with limited success. This was pointed out by Lane (172) and by several other investigators (253). This is primarily due to two reasons. The first is non-inclusion of sediment load as one of the independent variables in the equations along with Q and d. This has been pointed out by Lane and others. The second reason is that, as pointed out by Blench, and Simons and Albertson (253) since, in Indian canals in the north, the bank material has cohesivity, Lacey's equations are applicable to canals with sandy bed and cohesive banks. In spite of these limitations Lacey's contribution is considered to be one of the milestones in the progress of Fluvial Hydraulics (157). Later investigators who have worked on this problem have arrived at equations close to those of Lacey.

Lacey's equation for velocity $U = 18\, R^{2/3} S^{1/3}$ in fps units, or $\frac{U}{\sqrt{D}} = 18\,(D^{1/2} S)^{1/3}$ was based on data from sand bedded Indian canals and gravel and boulder rivers in India. Lacey and Pemberton (170) have produced a graph between $U/\sqrt{D}$ and $(D^{1/2} S)^{1/3}$ for active or bankful stage. A unique curve has been obtained on log-log scale with constant slope in different size-range of bed material e.g. the slope of curve n changes with sediment size as follows:

		n
less than 0.06 mm	:	1.0
0.06 to 0.20 mm	:	0.50
0.20 to 2.00 mm	:	0.33
greater than 2.00 mm	:	0.25

Sir Claude Cavendish Inglis (1983-1974) was born in Dublin in 1883 and was educated in Dublin and in England (264). In 1906 he was appointed in the Indian Services of Engineers and was posted in Sind as assistant engineer on the Jamrao canal. He was transferred to Bombay Presidency in 1911 and continued to work there till 1937 in the capacities of executive engineer, superintending engineer and then in charge of Irrigation Development and Research Circle. During this period he was in charge of Godavari canals and Neera canal and then he was dealing with soil classification, land drainage, land reclamation and related research. When he was responsible for river gauging, he developed the flood formula for flood discharge as a function of the catchment area. He also gave advice on the problems related to Sukkur barrage design, design of hydraulic structures, sediment excluders and foundation problem of Hardinge bridge. These were based on model studies conducted at research station in Khadakwasla near Pune, India. When the decision was taken to develop this research station into Central Irrigation and Hydrodynamic Research Station in 1937, Inglis was appointed as its first director on which position he continued till 1945 when he retired at the age of sixty three. During this period several specific investigations were conducted about training of rivers for barrages and bridges, and bank protection by spurs. Advice was also given on the flood problem and migration of the Kosi and sediment problem in Calcutta port. Several basic studies in Fluvial Hydraulics were also conducted. After his retirement the Government of India commissioned him to write a report on the research conducted at Khadakwasla. This report (139) was published in 1949 under the title "Behaviour and Control of Rivers and Canals with the Aid of Models", and contains a wealth of information useful for river engineers.

Claude Cavendish Inglis
(1883-1974)

Inglis was appointed the first director of Wallingford Research Station in 1947 when it was established in U.K. He was sixty four years old at that time. He was responsible for selecting the site, finalising the layout, planning the facilities and initiating the research in various aspects of Hydraulics. He was elected as Fellow of the Royal Society. He retired from Wallingford Research Station at the age of 75. Inglis was active in consulting work almost throughout after his retirement; he died in 1974.

Inglis was impressed by Lacey's paper on Stable Channels and both cooperated and exchanged ideas on regime method of channel design. Lacey's f_1 was only a function of sediment size. Inglis pointed out that different values are obtained for the Lacey silt factor when computed from various equations proposed by him viz., f_1 (U, R), f_1 (R, S) and f_1 (U, R, S) for stable channels, a fact later indicated by Ning Chien and others. Inglis (139) proposed a set of regime equations (taking clue from C.M. White's work) which involved sediment concentration as one of the variables. However, the constants in these equations need to be evaluated. During his tenure in Khadakwasla several investigations were conducted in the area of Fluvial Hydraulics. Experiments were conducted in a flume to study ripple formation and a qualitative explanation was given for it. The concept of dominant discharge was introduced by him. Field data on meander geometry were collected and analysed and empirical relationships were obtained between meander length M_L and meander belt M_B as a function of the width or the bankful discharge in the form

$$M_L \text{ or } M_B = \text{Const. } Q^{1/2}$$

where Q is the bankful discharge. Field data on scour at bridge piers were collected and the scour depth below the water surface was related to Lacey's depth. Procedure for design of distorted river models with movable beds, using regime equations was developed and used. Recommendations, based on laboratory and field experience, were made for location of spurs for bank protection and river training. Tidal models were also designed and tested.

His writings indicate that under not so favourable environment, as far as research is concerned, Inglis did a remarkable job in river training, bank protection, meandering and sediment exclusion. Later D.V Joglekar, who was trained under Inglis, continued work at the Central Water & Power Research Station, Khadakwasla. However, this work related to solving specific river training problems rather than exploring new areas of research. Later under the guidance of Joglekar, the "Manual on River Behaviour, Training and Control" was published by CBIP, India, as Publ. No. 60, 1956. This publication gives the state of art in River behaviour and control as understood and practised in India at that time.

Discussion about regime approach would not be complete without mentioning about Thomas Blench and his contributions. Blench graduated in Civil Engineering and Mechanics from the University of Glasgow in 1927 and obtained D.Sc. from the University of Alberta (Canada), in 1959. During 1927-1948 he worked for the Irrigation Department of Public Works Department of Punjab (India) and was involved in the construction and maintenance of irrigation works, control of irrigation, river observation and river engineering. He joined the University of

Thomas Blench
(1906-1993)

Alberta in 1948 and worked there till 1971 when he became the Professor Emeritus there. In addition to the teaching and research activities, he was also engaged in consultation work related to river engineering, hydrology, hydraulic structures and related fields. At Alberta he developed a viable research programme in the area of regime analysis of rivers and channels. Several students and associates working with him later contributed to the development of regime approach; these include R.B. Erb, M.A. Qureshi, R.H. Cooper, A.W. Peterson, V.J. Galay and G. Parker. He died in October 1993 at the age of eighty seven.

In 1941, Blench and King (27) proposed that Lacey's silt factor f_1 needs to be replaced by a bed factor F_b and a side factor F_s when bed and bank materials are different. They also recommended the use of average water surface width W and average depth D in place of perimeter P and hydraulic radius R. They defined the bed factor $F_b = U^2/D$ and the side factor $F_s = U^3/W$; they found that for regime channels

$$U^2 / gDS = 3.63\,(UW/\nu)^{0.25} \tag{55}$$

Blench gave the following design equations in terms of discharges Q, F_b and F_s, in SI units

$$\left.\begin{aligned} W &= \sqrt{F_b/F_s}\;Q^{1/2} \\ D &= (F_s/F_b^2)^{1/3}\;Q^{1/3} \\ S &= \frac{F_b^{5/6}\,F_s^{1/12}\,\nu^{1/4}}{1.91\,g\,Q^{1/6}} \end{aligned}\right\} \tag{56}$$

Later, on the basis of Gilbert's data, slope equation was modified to include bed-load concentration $\overline{C}_B$ in ppm by weight.Thus in SI units, the slope equation had the form

$$\left.\begin{aligned} S &= \frac{F_b^{5/6}\,F_s^{1/12}\,\nu^{1/4}}{11.91\,g\,Q^{1/6}\,(1+\overline{C}_B/2333)} \\ F_b &= F_{bo}\,(1+0.012\,\overline{C}_B),\; F_{bo} = 1.9\sqrt{d} \end{aligned}\right\} \tag{57}$$

with d in mm, F_s values varied between 0.10–0.30 for finer material and for coarse rounded material $F_s = \sqrt{d}/4$, with d in mm. Later Blench applied regime equations to the rivers using bankful discharge conditions. In addition to the research publications, Blench wrote the following three books to disseminate regime concepts

- Regime Behaviour of Canals and Rivers. Butterworth, London, 1957.
- Mobile Bed Fluviology. University of Alberta Press, Edmonton, (Canada), 1969.
- Mechanics of Plains Rivers: A Regime Theory Treatment of Canals and Rivers for Environmental Engineers. Printing Services University of Alberta, Edmonton (Canada) 1986.

It may be mentioned that in the light of present day concepts in fluid mechanics and the mechanics of sediment transport, one may disagree with the explanations, concepts and theorisation proposed by Lacey, Inglis and Blench.However, the zeal and dedication with which they continued to work even in the advanced age is truly commendable. Further recent analysis of stable channels have yielded equations very close to those proposed by Lacey.

Meandering

During the period under consideration attempts were made to understand the mechanics of meander formation and to obtain empirical relationships for the meander length M_L and meander belt M_B. Experiments were conducted by Forchheimer (82) 1926, Vogel and Thompson in 1933, Quaraishy (230) 1943, Friedkin (86) 1945, and Inglis (139) 1949. Experiments carried out by Friedkin and Inglis were on fairly large scale. The objective of these experiments was to know the conditions under which meanders develop and mechanics of their formation. Data from rivers were also collected earlier by Jefferson, and Griggs, and later by Inglis and others. Analysis of these data broadly confirmed that M_L and M_B are proportional to $Q^{1/2}$, where Q is mean annual or dominant discharge, and hence M_L and M_B are nearly proportional to river width. Several theories were put forward to explain why the rivers meander.These include (i) earth's rotation theory suggested by Gilbert in 1884, and Quaraishy (230) 1943; (ii) disturbance theory by Griggs (113) 1906, Hjulstrom, Friedkin (86) 1945, Tiffnay (268) 1941, and Werner (286) 1951, (iii) helicoidal flow theory by Prus-Chacincky, and Leliavsky (184) 1954; and (iv) excess energy theory by Schoklitsch, Inglis, and later by Joglekar (38) 1956, and Leopold and Wolman (186) 1960. These were really not the theories but qualitative explanations indicating the conditions under which meander formation takes place. Each one of these conditions may produce meandering but it was not the only condition under which meanders formed. It was only in 60's and 70's that a more theoretical analysis of meander formation was attempted using stability analysis.

CONTRIBUTIONS FROM OTHER COUNTRIES

The above discussion is based primarily on the published literature in English and some in French and German. During the Eighth Congress of IAHR held in 1959 at Montreal a seminar on Transport of Materials in water was held (136). In this seminar Regional Reports on Transport of Material in water were presented for Japan, France, Central Europe and the USSR.These reports give some idea about the work done in these regions during the 1930-1958 approximately.

In Japan Kurihara, and Iwagaki studied the problem of critical tractive stress theoretically and experimentally. Scour due to horizontal jet was studied by Kurihara who showed that (scour length/ nozzle diameter) is a function of $U / \sqrt{\Delta\gamma_s\, d / \rho_f}$. Scour due to vertical jets was studied by Awazu. Bed form characteristics and their formation were studied by Kinoshita, Hayashi and Yatsu, Matsunashi, Yano and Adachi, and Tsubaki. It was shown that dimensionless Chezy coefficient depends on R/K_s where K_s is greater than the bed material size and K_s/d is a function of $\tau_o / (\gamma_s - \gamma_f)\, d$ and Froude number. It was shown by Shimura that Karman constant in a stream with suspended load is smaller than 0.40 and obtained expression for it. Sediment transport formulae were developed by Sato, Kikkawa and Ashida.

In Russia considerable amount of work was done on all aspects of Fluvial Hydraulics (166). Extensive experimental investigations were carried out in 1935-1936 by V.N. Goncharov, G.N. Lapshin and V.V. Roborovskaya using sediments of diameters varying from 0.35 mm to 12 mm to determine the non-transporting velocity and velocities of initial formation and greatest formation of dunes. Levi showed that non-transporting velocity in dimensionless form i.e. $U_c / \sqrt{\Delta\gamma_s\, d / \rho_f}$ is proportional to $\log \frac{D}{d}$. Egiazaroff in 1950 showed that the coefficient of proportionality between these two parameters is dependent $d\sqrt{\Delta\gamma_s\, d / \rho_f} / \nu$ and is constant only when the bed is hydrodynamically rough.

V.F. Pushkarev in 1936 carried out experiments to predict mean velocity of flow in channels. Under the guidance of M.A. Velikanov, B.A. Fidman and N.A. Mikhailova worked on the turbulence structure in open channel flows. V.S. Knoroz in 1951 conducted investigations on the bed-load transport under dune bed condition. These have been followed by investigations of N.S. Zamenskaya in 1956 and A.F. Kudryashov in 1957. These studies have yielded expressions for dune height. Simultaneously, as reporte d by G.V. Lopatin, data on dune dimensions and their velocity were collected in the rivers Volga, Mologa, Luga and Kemka during 1934-1935. These studies indicated the importance of Froude number in the formation and movement of dunes.

Earliest studies on flow in channel bends were those by A.Ya. Milovich in 1914 to determine the trajectories of bottom and surface particles. The investigations by N.F. Daneliya in 1936 were carried out in 30°, 90° and 150° bends at one velocity and depth to determine the velocity distributions. In 1949, M.P. Kozhevnikov carried out a wide range of experiments to study the form of free surface and the trajectories of bottom and surface currents in bends. Then in 1940-50 I.L. Rozovskii carried out detailed investigations of flow in bends. Field observations on bends in the Volga river were made by A.K. Proskuryakov in 1940. In 1950, similar studies were carried out by K.I. Rossinskii and N.A. Kuzmin on the Klyazma river. Large-scale experiments on meandering were carried out by O.A. Andreev and I.A. Yaroslavtev. Their objective was the same as of Freidkin's work. Side by side the theory of secondary circulation was developed by a number of investigators including N.E. Zhukovskii, V.M. Makkaveev, M.V. Potapov, A.K. Ananyan and others.

Experiments on the channel processes and channel morphology were carried out during 1948-1951 under the guidance of M.A.Velikanov.These provided the morphological dimensionless parameters viz. B/d, H/d and $Q/d^2\sqrt{\Delta\gamma_s d/\rho_f}$, their inter-relationship being of the form

$$\frac{B}{d} \text{ or } \frac{H}{d} = \text{const. } (Q/d^2 \sqrt{\Delta\gamma_s d/\rho_f})^p$$

Later Velikanov also suggested equations of the type

$$\frac{B}{d} \text{ or } \frac{H}{d} = \text{const. } (Q/d^2 \sqrt{gds})^p$$

where p = 0.50 to 0.53 for B/d relation and 0.25 to 0.27 for H/d relation. Several other morphological studies were also carried out. Here H is the flow depth.

The differential form of continuity equation for the sediment

$$\frac{\partial}{\partial t}(ZB) + \frac{1}{\gamma_s}\frac{\partial Q_B}{\partial x} = 0$$

was obtained by Bernadsky in 1932. Sediment discharge formulae were developed by Goncharov, Levi, Egiazaroff and others. The continuity equation along with sediment transport law, resistance law, continuity equation and back water equation were used by Levi and Sapihr in 1948 to study deformation of river bed in unsteady non-uniform flows. Sediment diffusion equation was obtained by Mackaveyev in 1932. Local scour was studied by Izbach, Patrashev and Kumin.

In East European countries namely Czechoslovakia, Hungary, Bulgaria, Poland and Rumania work on incipient motion of sediment, sediment transport, roughness and resistance was carried out but no details are available.

In 1935, Hjulstrom (128) from Uppsala presented a diagram of U vs. d on which erosion, transportation and deposition regions were identified.Tison studied critical stress condition for uniform material. He also performed experiments on various sized materials to study the ripple dimensions. Pang (218) 1939 studied the critical tractive stress of flat materials.

During 30's and early 40's many Chinese students did their doctoral work in European and American universities who later went back to China and made significant contributions in solving sediment problems. These included Chetty Ho, Yun-Chang Tu and Te-Yun Liu (sediment transport studies at Iowa), T.L. Chou and Y.L. Chang (bed transport and modelling of river problem at Manchester), S.D. Chyn (sediment transport at MIT), P.Y. Ho (stable channels at Univ. of London),

C.C. Wang (Suspended load transport at Karlsruhe), Ning Chien (Sediment Transport at Berkeley), C.L. Pien (Turbulence and suspended material transport at Iowa), C.S. Hsia (Transport of fine sediment at Iowa), and Bingnan Lin (Effect of concentration on fall velocity, at Iowa).

The US Waterways Experiment Station was established at Vicksburg (Miss), USA in 1929 with Lt. H.D. Vogel as its first director. Work carried here in 1930s on Studies of River Bed Materials and Their Movement with Special Reference to the Lower Mississippi, 1935 is often quoted. Later many aspects of river hydraulics were studied at WES. It may be mentioned that Freidkin's work on Meandering was carried out in WES.

CONCLUDING REMARKS

The period 1925-50 saw considerable progress in Fluvial Hydraulics. Laboratories were extensively used to study complex problems of incipient-motion and bed-load and suspended load transport, flow in bends and morphological processes. As a result Shields' criterion for incipient motion, bed-load equations of Meyer-Peter and Müller, Kalinske, and Einstein, and suspended concentration distribution equations were developed which formed the basis of Fluvial Hydraulics. Similarly, the concept of dividing total resistance to flow into grain resistance and form resistance was introduced by Einstein and his co-workers and a method was developed for predicting resistance. In all these developments more and more use was made of fluid mechanics principles. Regime method of channel design which was introduced by Kennedy and Lindley was further developed by Lacey on one side and Blench on other side using somewhat different approaches. However, its limitations were also indicated by Lane and others. Meander formation studies were conducted in laboratory and field data were utilited to obtain empirical equations for M_L and M_B. Another significant contribution was to develop a frame work of governing equations for computation of bed profiles in unsteady nonuniform flows. However, computation of the profiles was hampered because of time consuming computational work using desk calculators that were available at that time. Lastly in this period Fluvial Hydraulics was recognised as an important branch of hydraulics as can be seen from the fact that one chapter in Engineering Hydraulics edited by Rouse was devoted to sediment transport.

Chapter 7

Developments During 1950–1975

As mentioned earlier, the basic foundations of the sediment transport theory and governing equations of motion were established by 1950, namely critical tractive stress analysis of Shields, bed-load transport formulae of Meyer-Peter and Müller, and Einstein, and suspended load distribution theory of Rouse and Ippen. Further, comprehensive method of computation of total load was also proposed by Einstein.

The next twenty five years witnessed remarkable increase in the research activity in the area of Fluvial Hydraulics. After the Second World War several programmes were available for the exchange of scientists, scholars and students from Asia to Europe and USA, and between the USA and European countries. This helped in the exchange of ideas, development of expertise and starting of new centres of research. Journal of Hydraulics Division of the A S C E, and biennial Congress proceedings of IAHR became the primary publications for reporting the research findings. The geologists, geomorphologists and geographers got interested in the applied aspects of Fluvial Hydraulics and made significant contributions in such aspects as gravel-bed streams, channel adjustments, plan forms and effect of land slides, floods and tectonics on river morphology.

Realising the complexities of all Fluvial Hydraulic phenomena, there was concerted effort to collect reliable data from flume studies, stable channels and rivers. As examples, one can mention United States Geological Survey programmes of collecting data from flume studies at Fort Collins and field data from sandy streams in USA, Central Board of Irrigation and Power (India) programme of collection of canal data, and Canal Headworks Operation Programme (CHOP) in Pakistan on stable channels. There was tendency to use as many data as available from laboratory and field to obtain the relevant relationships. Hence compendiums of data on resistance, sediment transport and scour were prepared and used.

It was also during this period that computers were available to research engineers and scientists, and hence complex problems involving partial nonlinear differential equations of irregular channel sections were solved developing complex computer programmes. Hence great strides were made in the analysis of aggradation and degradation problems. Also, with the availability of computers, use of optimisation principles in Fluvial Hydraulics was possible and was attempted in the case of channel design and plan form adjustment.

Lastly, Fluvial Hydraulics began taking shape into a well defined branch of hydraulics with lot of potential in application to real life problems and further development. As a result the Fluvial Hydraulics or Erosion and Sedimentation was taught as one of the subjects in Civil Engineering at graduate level, in many universities, and relatively a large number of reports, lecture notes and books were published on the subject.

SEDIMENT MOVEMENT AND TRANSPORT

Yuichi Iwagaki
(1923-)

Dr. Yuichi Iwagaki (1923–) was born in Japan in 1923 and received his bachelor's and doctoral degrees from the University of Kyoto, Japan in 1946 and 1956, respectively. Starting his research career as a research assistant at Kyoto University in 1949, he rose to the rank of Professor in 1960 and after retirement he is working as a Professor in the Meijo University at Nagoya, Japan. He has contributed extensively in the areas of open channel flow, Fluvial Hydraulics, hydrology and coastal processes. In Fluvial Hydraulics, he has made significant contributions in raindrop erosion, use of method of characteristics for computing river bed variations, analysis of critical tractive stress of noncohesive materials and gravels, stable channel cross-sectional profiles, scour from jets and wall jets, and open channel friction at high Froude numbers.

Iwagaki (145) 1956 carried out theoretical and experimental analysis of incipient motion of sedimentary particles by evaluating the motivating and resisting forces using boundary layer theory. His analysis is by far the most comprehensive one. Later he and Tsuchiya studied the critical motion condition of gravel materials. Critical velocity approach was used by Neill, and Garde who showed that when viscous effects are negligible, critical mean velocity U_c is given by $U_c \Big/ \sqrt{\frac{\Delta\gamma_s}{\rho_f} d} = f(R/d)$. It was realised that the analysis of Shields and others is applicable to nearly uniform materials. Critical tractive stress for nonuniform materials was studied by Egiazaroff (71) 1965, Ashida and Michiue (14) 1971, and

Hayashi et al. (124) 1980, who showed that $\tau_{*ci} / \tau_{*ca} = f(d_i / d_a)$, where τ_{*ci} and τ_{*ca} are the dimensionless critical tractive stresses for size d_i and arithmetic mean size d_a respectively.

It was realised that the analysis by Shields and others, which used either critical tractive stress or critical velocity approach, was not applicable to cohesive materials in which case the residual electric charges, which can be either +ve or –ve, impart to the soil an ability to hold certain cations or anions. Experimental studies were conducted by Dunn (58) 1959, Smerdon and Beasley (254) 1961, Partheniades (225) 1970 and others to find out the other factors on which the critical tractive stress for cohesive materials would depend. However, no conclusive recommendations were in sight.

BED-LOAD TRANSPORT

This period saw intense activity in the area of sediment transport. Einstein and Ning Chien (66) 1953 reported experiments on bed-load transport using sediment with large standard deviation. Sato, Kikkawa and Ashida (244) 1958, also showed the importance of resistance in sediment transport phenomenon. They found that $q_B / \tau_* u_* f(\tau_o / \tau_{oc}) = (1/40\, n)^{3.5}$ for $n \leq 0.025$ and is equal to unity for $n > 0.025$. Rottner (234) 1959 analysed the bed-load data from the consideration of transport as well as the resistance and produced a unified graph between

$$U \Big/ \sqrt{\frac{\Delta\gamma_s d}{\rho_f}}, \quad q_B \Big/ \gamma_s \sqrt{\frac{\gamma_s - \gamma_f}{\gamma_f}} \sqrt{gD^3}, \quad \frac{S}{\Delta\gamma_s / \gamma_f} \text{ and } \frac{D}{d}.$$

Bharat Singh (24, 25) conducted experiments and obtained Meyer-Peter Müller type equation. Garde and Albertson (91) 1961 showed the importance of bed-forms and resistance on the bed-load transport by plotting $q_B / (\gamma_s u_* d)$ vs $\tau_0 / (\gamma_s - \gamma_f) d$ and U/u_*. Whereas for the plane bed data, a unique curve was obtained between $q_B / (\gamma_s u_* d)$ and $\tau_0 / (\gamma_s - \gamma_f) d$, for the dune bed data, points with constant value of U/u_* fell on a single curve. Yalin (292, 293) expressed transport rate as the rate of doing work and wrote $q_B = W_s u_s$ where W_s is the weight of solids moving on the unit area of the bed at velocity u_s. On this basis, he developed an equation which takes the functional form

$$q_B / (\gamma_s u_* d) = f\left(\frac{\tau_o - \tau_{oc}}{\tau_{0c}}, \frac{\tau_o}{(\gamma_s - \gamma_f) d}, \frac{\tau_{oc}}{(\gamma_s - \gamma_f) d}\right)$$

Brig. Ralph A. Bagnold, FRS (1896-1990) was born in April 1896 in Davenport, England (267). He was commissioned in Royal Engineers in 1915 and spent most of his army career in the Corps of Signals. After the First World War, Bagnold was given study leave when he went to Cambridge (U.K.) and obtained degree in Engineering from Malvern College in 1921. During 1921-1935 he was posted in Ireland, to Maresfiled Park and then in Egypt. During 1926-1932 Bagnold began a series of expeditions in unmapped regions of Sinai, Baluchistan, Persia and

Ralph A. Bagnold
(1896-1990)

Libyan desert where he was greatly interested in the formation of desert dunes. When he retired from the army in 1935, he conducted a series of experiments in a wind tunnel to study the physics of dune formation. In 1939, he wrote a book on "Physics of Blown Sand and Desert Dunes" which is still a valuable source of information, almost 60 years after its first publication.

Bagnold was recalled to the army in 1939 immediately after the Second World War broke out. After the war was over, Bagnold returned to his academic pursuits and studied resistance to the flow and sediment transport. He was invited to the US Geological Survey for interacting with the hydraulic engineers there. This led to the publication of papers on river meanders and use of stream power in the sediment transport analysis. The themes of his publications after 1940 included beach formation by waves, waves in shallow water, movement of cohesionless grains by flowing water, formation of sand dunes, gravity force dispersion of large solid spheres in Newtonian fluid under shear, flow in sinuous channels, river meanders, sediment discharge and stream power, an approach to the sediment transport problem from general physics, saltation and bed-load transport, and sediment transport by wind and water. He remained active and continued to publish till his end which came in May 1990 at the age of 95.

Bagnold (15, 16) approached the problem of bed-load transport from physics point of view. He reasoned that the submerged weight of the solids in motion must be supported by the momentum transfer from solids or from fluid to solid, or both and then related the work done to the available power supply per uniy area ($\tau_o U$) commonly known as stream power. Bagnold's approach ultimately gives an expression for total load.

It may be mentioned in passing that only Einstein's bed-load equation gives the size distribution of bed-load transport. Other equations developed so far were either for uniform or nearly uniform material and had ignored the effect of non-uniformity. Ashida and Michiue (14) 1973 have obtained a relation between $\frac{d_i}{d_m}$, $\frac{\tau_o}{(\gamma_s - \gamma_f)\, d_i}$ and $\frac{i_B\, q_B}{\gamma_s\, u'_*\, i_b\, d_i}$. Here, u'_* is shear velocity with reference to grain and d_m is median size of bed material. Also i_b the fraction of bed material of size d_i and $i_B q_B$ represents the bed-load of that size.

SUSOPENDED LOAD TRANSPORT

The basic equation for distribution of suspended sediment concentration in the vertical in steady unform, flow had already been developed, viz.,

$$\frac{C}{C_a} = \left(\frac{D-y}{y}\,\frac{a}{D-a}\right)^{Z_0} \tag{43}$$

where $Z_0 = \omega_0 / u_* \kappa$. From some available data from laboratory and field it was found that the observed value of the exponent Z did not agree with $Z_0 = \omega_0 / u_* \kappa$. Hence, during this period, efforts were made to refine the theory and find plausible explanations for this discrepancy. Hunt (134) 1954, considered the space occupied by sediment particles suspended in a fluid and obtained an expression for concentration C. Einstein and Chien (67, 68) suggested six second approximations to the suspended sediment concentration distribution theory by modifying some of the assumptions made in the derivation of Eq. (43). Tanaka and Sugimoto (263) 1958 refined the logarithmic velocity distribution law by assuming $\tau = \tau_0 \left(1 - \frac{y}{D}\right)$ instead of $\tau = \tau_0$ and improved Eq. (43). Navntoft (206) 1970 treated sediment water complex as one phase flow with density variation and proposed a logarithmic relation for concentration at any distance y from the bed as

$$C = B_2 \ln \left[\frac{A_2 + \frac{y}{D}}{A_2 + \left(\frac{y}{D}\right)_{C=0}}\right]$$

where A_2 and B_2 are empirical constants and $(y/D)_{C=0}$ is the relative depth at which $C = 0$. Ippen (141) 1971, proposed a relation

$$\frac{C}{C_a} = \left(\frac{D-y}{y+a} \cdot \frac{2a}{D}\right)^{Z_2}$$

where elevation "a" above the bed is given by

$$u_s / u_* = \frac{u_* a}{\nu} \ln \left(1 + \frac{D}{a}\right)$$

and $Z_2 = \frac{\omega_0}{\beta u_*} \cdot \frac{u_*' a}{\nu}$. The observed exponent Z_1 was found to be $Z_1 = \frac{Z_2}{1 + 0.6\, Z_2}$.

Lavelle and Thacker (181) 1978, considered the effect of concentration on the fall velocity of suspended particles and also a new distribution for the sediment transfer coefficient. Inspite of these efforts, there was not significant improvement in the distribution in some cases; in other cases the new equations needed extensive verification which was not available. Hence, inspite of certain limitations of Eq. (43), it is being used very often.

Other aspects of Eq. (43) that needed consideration were prediction of the reference concentration C_a and limits of integration of this equation. These aspects were considered by Garde (90) 1959, Brooks (32) 1963, and Harrison and Lidicker (118) 1963.

Analysis of non-equilibrium transport of suspended sediment was initiated by Kalinske in 1940. More progress was made in this area during the period under consideration. Assuming u and ε_s to remain constant over the depth and $\varepsilon_s = \bar{\varepsilon}$ and $u = U$ the diffusion equation for two dimensional flow becomes

$$U \frac{\partial C}{\partial x} = \bar{\varepsilon} \frac{\partial^2 C}{\partial y^2} + \omega_0 \frac{\partial C}{\partial y} \tag{46}$$

This equation has been solved numerically by Apmann and Rumer (9) 1970 and analytically by Mei (199) 1969 using Laplace Transform technique. Kerssens and Van Rijn (160) 1977 have solved this equation for variable ε_s.

Ning Chien
(1922-1986)

Ning Chien (1922-1986) was born in Hangzhou, China in 1922. He graduated with B.S. in Civil Engineering in 1943, from the Central University, China, and went to USA for further studies. In the USA, he received M.S. from the University of Iowa in 1948 and Ph.D. from the University of California, Berkeley in 1951. His Ph.D. dissertation supervised by Prof. H.A. Einstein was titled "Investigation of the Maximum Equilibrium Rate of Bed-Load Movement". He worked with Prof. Einstein upto 1955 after which he returned to China and became research fellow in the Institute of Hydrotechnical Research of Academia Sinica; later he was appointed as Deputy Head of Sedimentation Engineering Department of the Institute of Water Conservancy and Hydroelectric Power Research in Beijing. Between 1973-1986, he was professor of Hydraulic Engineering at Tsinghua University, Beijing and Head of the Sedimentation Laboratory. He passed away in December 1986 after a prolonged illness.

Ning Chien initiated the study on Flow at Hyperconcentrations of sediment as it occurs in the Yellow river and is considered to be pioneer of modern school of Fluvial Hydraulics in China. During his active life, he published a large number of papers in the area of Fluvial Hydraulics, both basic and applied in nature. His contributions are related to transport of sediment mixtures with large spreads and sizes, wash-load, refinements in the solution of suspended load theory, effects of heavy sediment concentration on velocity and sediment distributions, similarity laws for river models with movable beds, inclusion of sediment load as a factor in regime relationships, effect of water temperature on sediment motion, morphology of the Yellow river, regulation of braided streams, two phase flows, channel pattern formation, and effect of reservoirs on channel morphology. Most of his later publications are in Chinese. Ning Chien has published five books in Chinese on the following aspects of Fluvial Hydraulics.

1. Density Currents. Water Resources and Electric Power Press, 1957.
2. Similarity Laws of Distorted River Model with Movable Bed. Science Publishing House, 1957.
3. Fluvial Processes of the Lower Yellow River. Science Publishing House, 1965.
4. Mechanics of Sediment Transport. Science Publishing House, 1983.
5. Fluvial Processes. Science Publishing House, 1987.

Another major contribution of Ning Chien was the organisation of the First International Symposium on River Sedimentation in China in 1980 and the establishment of International Research and Training Centre on Erosion and Sedimentation in Beijing in 1984. This Centre strives to have regional cooperation in research and training in Fluvial Hydraulics.

Bingnan Lin
(1920-)

Another Chinese Engineer whose mention should be made here is Bingnan Lin (1920–) who was born in Malaya in 1920 and obtained his first degree in Civil Engineering from the Chiao Tung University in China in 1942. He obtained his M.S. and Ph.D. from University of Iowa in 1947 and 1951 respectively. Later he worked as Assistant Professor at Colorado State University, Fort Collins (USA) during 1952–1955 and returned to China in 1955, where he held various positions in the Institute of Hydraulic Research, Academia Sinica, Institute of Water Conservancy and Hydroelectric Power Research (IWHR), Tsinghua University and then as Director, IWHR and Chief Scientist of the Sedimentation Specialist Group for Three Gorges Project.

Lin's contributions to Fluvial Hydraulics relate to numerical analysis of unsteady flows in open channels; effect of sediment concentration on the fall velocity; roughness and sediment transport studies; geometry of stable channels; sediment problems in the estuaries of the Hai, Yellow, Pearl and Qiantag Rivers; mathematical modelling in alluvial streams, and unsteady transport of suspended load. Along with Ning Chien, Lin also played an important role in the International

Cooperative Project on Research and Training in Erosion and Sedimentation and starting an International Journal on Sediment Research.

TOTAL LOAD

Einstein's method of computation of total sediment load was applied to a few streams in the USA and it was found that the method does not give accurate results for shallow sandy streams. Hence Einstein's method was modified by Colby, Hembree and Schroeder (47, 247) during 1955-1956, by using some measured quantities and introducing some corrections of empirical nature in Einstein's procedure. Some modifications were also suggested by Toffaleti (270) 1969. Thus, Toffaleti split suspended sediment distribution curve in three regions of depth and proposed power type relationship for each. As against these methods of microrcopic nature in which suspended load and bed-load are computed separately and added, some macroscopic methods were also proposed in which dimensionless total transport rate is related to a set of dimensionless parameters. Thus, the following functional relationships were proposed

Laursen (180) 1958, $\overline{C}_T \Big/ \left(\frac{d}{D}\right)^{7/6} \left(\frac{\tau_0'}{\tau_{oc}} - 1\right) = f(u_*/\omega_0)$

Garde and Albertson (88) 1958, $\overline{C}_T = f\left(\frac{u_* d}{\nu}, \frac{\omega_o d}{\nu}, \frac{d}{D}\right)$

Garde and Dattatri (92) 1963, $q_T/\gamma_s\, u_*\, d = f(\tau_0/(\gamma_s - \gamma_f)\, d)$

Frank A. Engelund
(1925-1983)

Engelund and Hansen (75) 1967, postulated that in the case of a duned bed, the moving sediment particle was elevated through the dune height h. The energy required for elevating the sediment load (per unit time per unit width) is $\frac{q_T(\gamma_s - \gamma_s)\, h}{\gamma_s}$. This must be equal to the work done by the drag force on the particles. Assuming the particle velocity to be proportional to u_*, they obtained the equation $f\phi_T = 0.4\, \tau_*^{5/2}$ were f is the Darcy-Weisbach friction factor, τ_* is the dimensionless shear and ϕ_T is dimensionless transport rate. It is interesting to note that even though from the point of view of the mechanism proposed, the above equation should be valid for dune bed condition only, it is found to be valid for plane bed data also. It also needs to be pointed out that the proposed mechanism does not include suspension phenomenon properly.

Frank A. Engelund (1925-1983) was born in 1925 and graduated in 1948 from the Technical University of Denmark. After his graduation he worked for three years in the Hydraulics Laboratory of Technical University of Denmark. During 1953-1960 he worked as Consulting Engineer in the Field of Port Engineering. He started his academic career in 1959 as lecturer in Applied Mathematics at the Technical University of Denmark and rose to the level of Professor of Hydrodynamics and Hydraulic Engineering in 1963. He continued to work as professor for the next twenty years till his premature death in June 1983 at the age of 57.

E. Hansen, Engelund and his associate Jorgen Fredsoe have made important contributions to various aspects of Fluvial Hydraulics. These contributions reveal clearly Engelund's ability to formulate simple mathematical models for the fluvial processes and to validate them with available experimental data. Frank Engelund was greatly appreciated by his colleagues, friends and students for his warm and modest personality. After his demise, the school that he developed in the Technical University of Denmark continues to be in the fore front under the leadership of Jorgen Fredsoe.

Engelund, Hansen, and Fredsoe's contributions relate to hydraulic resistance of alluvial streams, sediment transport, dispersion of floating particles on the free surface, instability of erodible beds, dune dimensions under steady and unsteady flow conditions, transition from dune to plane bed, and instability leading to the formation of meanders and braids. In addition Engelund also worked on problems related to drainage, multiple wells, turbulent flows, and wind generated waves.

Engelund and Fredsoe have analytically studied the transition from dunes to plane bed in alluvial streams and have indicated the role played by the suspended sediment in the stability of bed. They have shown that the phase shift δ between bed form and local rate of sediment transport is made of two contributions— one contribution originates from internal friction of the fluid, which causes a phase shift between bed form and the tractive stress; the other contribution originates from the sediment transport and is due to finite settling velocity of suspended particles which induces a lag of transport rate compared with the tractive stress. The two contributions are usually of opposite nature. As a result of their investigation they have concluded that the stability boundary between dune and plane bed, depends on q_B/q_s ratio. Larger this ratio, larger is the Froude number at which the transition occurs and vice versa. Similarly lower the water temperature, smaller will be this ratio and lower will be the Froude number of transition.

They have also derived a new bed-load equation, taking into account the equation for velocity of particle moving as bed-load that is developed by Luque.

Ackers and White (2) 1973 have proposed an equation involving the sediment mobility parameter $F_1 = \left[u_*^{c_1} / \sqrt{\Delta\gamma_s\, d/\rho_f}\right] \left[U / \sqrt{32} \log (10\, D / d)\right]^{1 - c_1}$ and the sediment transport parameter, $S = (u_* / U)^{c_1} (\gamma_s / \gamma_f) (\overline{C}_T D / d)$ and obtained an equation of the form

$$S = C_2 \left[\frac{F_1}{C_3} - 1\right]^{C_4}$$

where c_1, c_2, c_3, and c_4, are the functions of dimensionless particle diameter $d_* = (\Delta\gamma_s / \rho_f v^2)^{1/3} d$.

Some other equations were also developed for predicting the total load transport in alluvial streams. A few more can be mentioned. Vittal, Ranga Raju and Garde (284) 1973, introduced the concept of effective shear stress which they defined as the shear stress which would be required on the plane bed to cause sediment transport rate equal to that observed on the duned bed. For bed-load transport it was equal to shear corresponding to grain roughness, as used by Einstein and others; however, it was found to be greater than τ_0' in the presence of suspended load Later $\tau_t / (\gamma_s - \gamma_f)\, d$ was found to be related to τ_*' and $(\tau_0'/\tau_0)^{-m}$ where $m = f\left(\frac{u_*}{\omega_0}\right)$. Shen and Hung (248) 1972 proposed a regression equation between $\overline{C}_T$ and Y_* where

$$Y_* = (US^{0.57} / \omega_0^{0.32})^{0.0075}$$

Yang (296) 1973 related concentration of total sediment load to $\omega_0\, d/v$, u_* / ω_0 and $(US - U_c S) / \omega_0$ the dimensionless excess stream power. This equation is found to give quite satisfactory results.

SAMPLING

Several suspended-load samplers and bed-material samplers were developed during this period. Depth integrating suspended-sediment wading-type hand sampler US DH-48 is useful for streams with small depth, whereas the 62-pound depth integrating suspended-sediment sampler US DH-49 can be lowered by crane and used up to a depth of 6.0 m. Point integrating suspended-sediment sampler US P-50 is a 300 pound electrically operated sampler for collection of suspended-sediment samples at any point below the surface of the stream; it is little over a metre long and is equipped with tail fins for its proper orientation as in the case of US DH-49. Automatic single stage suspended-sediment sampler is used for automatic collecton of sample from flashy intermittent streams at remote or not easily accessible streams. These samplers are shown in the adjoining figure. Also, piston type bed-material sampler US BMH-53, bed-material sampler US BM-54, and other samplers were developed for sampling the bed-material from the rivers and reservoirs.

Depth integrating suspended-sediment wading-type hand sampler, US DH-48

Depth-integrating suspended sediment sampler, US D-49, head open

Some suspended sediment samplers

Point-integrating suspended sediment sampler, US P-50

Automatic single-stage suspended sediment sampler

Some suspended sediment samplers

In addition, three other major developments in sediment sampling and analysis took place during this period. The first is that the visual accumulation tube was developed under the Cooperative Programme at University of Iowa and reported by Colby and Christesen (48, 274) 1957. It directly determines the size distribution of a sediment sample and works on the principle of determination of fall velocity distribution by determininig the settling rate. The other concerns the development of Helley Smith sampler for bed-load measurement (125). It works on the principle of pressure difference and is the modified version of Arnheim sampler. Lastly a method has been developed to estimate the rate of bed-load transport by tracking the bed undulation movement by sonic depth sounder. It is shown that

$$q_B = 1.32\, U_w (1 - \lambda)\, \bar{\xi}$$

where U_w is the velocity of propagation of bed wave, λ is the porosity and $\bar{\xi} = |Z - \bar{Z}|$ is the mean of absolute bed variations.

REGIMES OF FLOW AND CHANNEL RESISTANCE

One aspect of Fluvial Hydraulics which attracted the attention of engineers in this period was description and prediction of different bed-forms or regimes of flow. Gilbert had already shown that with increasing flow over material of a given size, one gets, ripples, dunes, flat bed and antidune regimes. Under USGS project Simons and Richardson conducted extensive series of experiments in laborotory flumes at Colorado State University, Fort Collins (USA) during 1956-61 and collected valuable data on regimes, resistance and transport. On the basis of analysis of these data Albertson, Simons and Richardson (4) 1958 proposed $\frac{u_* d}{\nu}$ *vs* $\frac{u_*}{\omega_0}$ criterion for regimes which worked well for flume data but was not successful in predicting regimes in streams. Garde and Albertson (89) 1959 proposed τ_* *vs* Fr criterion which reasonably predicted ripples and dunes, transition and antidune regimes for flume as well as field data. Later Garde and Ranga Raju proposed $\frac{R}{d}$ *vs* $\frac{S}{\Delta\gamma_s/\gamma_f}$ criterion which seems to work well for a large volume of flume and field data. Other criteria proposed during this period were U / u'_* *vs* Fr criterion by Engelund and Hansen, $\frac{gd}{u_*^2}$ *vs* d criterion by Bogardi, and $\tau_0\, U$ *vs* d criterion by Simons and Richardson.

Janos Bogardi
(1909-)

During this period Bogardi from Hungary also actively participated in the advancement of Fluvial Hydraulics. Janos Bogardi (1909–) was born in Torda, Hungary and graduated from Budapest Technical University in 1931. He received his M.S. Degree from University of Iowa in 1938 and later D.Sc. from Hungarian Academy of Sciences. Bogardi spent several years on river training and flood control projects on the Danube and its tributaries, and in hydrological and hydrologic research. He was Director of the Hungarian Hydrological Services and Head of the Hydraulics Laboratory. Since 1962 he was professor till his retirement. Bogardi has published profusely in Hungarian language on various aspects of Fluvial Hydraulics, viz sediment loads of Hungarian rivers, suspended sediment transport, channel stability, analysis of hydraulic models with movable beds, and regimes of flow. His book entitled "Sediment Transport in Alluvial Streams" was first published in Hungarian language by the Hungarian Academy of Sciences in 1971 and was later translated in to English in 1978. His paper on "European Concepts of Sediment Transportation" in JHD, Proc. ASCE in 1965 and the above mentioned book contain valuable information about the developments in Fluvial Hydraulics in the former USSR and East European countries and data about sediment transport on some Hungarian rivers.

Maurice Lee Albertson (1918-)

Maurice Lee Albertson (1918-) from Kansas with degrees from the Iowa State University and the Iowa University worked at T.V.A. and then joined the Iowa Instiute of Hydraulic Research where he built wind tunnel and studied atmospheric diffusion. He was invited to the Colorado State University, Fort Collins (USA) in 1947 in the capacity of Professor and Head of Fluid Mechanics. Along with J.E. Cermak and others he developed extensive laboratory facilities there for research in Fluid Mechanics and Fluvial Hydraulics. In the field of Fluvial Hydraulics, E.W. Lane, D.B. Simons, E.V. Richardson and later H.W. Shen were associated. Under a series of master's and doctoral theses he investigated problems concerning fall velocity as affected by particle shape, stable channels, resistance, sediment transport, and scour. It was shown that the particle shape can be characterized by $c / \sqrt{ab}$ and that $C_D = f\,(Re,\; c / \sqrt{ab}\,)$; here $a, b, c,$ are the major, intermediate and minor axis of the particle and C_D is the drag coefficient. His contribution about prediction of regimes has been already discussed earlier. Under his supervision, regime channel data were collected by Simons and Bender and analysed. Albertson and others (23) 1955, also devised a novel method for measuring total load in the Niobrara river by throwing bed-load in suspension using artificial roughness and measuring the suspended load concentration.

Hsieh Wen Shen (1931-) a native of China, after studying the undergraduate engineering at Michigan, obtained his doctorate in sediment transport under H.A. Einstein at Berkeley and joined Colorado State University in 1964. He left C.S.U. in 1984 and joined University of California, Berkeley. He has done extensive studies on scour around bridge piers, transport of total load, development of bed roughness, spectral properties of bed forms and their velocity of propagation, stochastic modelling of bed-load on flat beds, meandering and braiding of channels, shear distribution in channel bends, transport of coal in pipe lines, variation of Einstein's hiding factor for the transport of non uniform sediment, and degradation. In this work, G.X. Chen, J.Y. Lu, H.F. Cheong, C.S. Hung , S. Vedula and others were associated. He has also edited two volumes of a book on River Mechanics which is an excellent source of information on various aspects of Fluvial Hydraulics.

The effect of presence of suspended sediment and bed undulations on the resistance to flow were studied by Nomicos (213) 1958 and it was shown that only when the bed is flat, significant reduction in friction factor takes place in the presence of sediment; the reduction is minimal in the presence of dunes. Brooks (31) 1958 through carefully collected data showed that in an alluvial stream, for given D, d and S, i.e for given $\tau_0 / (\gamma_s - \gamma_f)\, d$, one can get three velocities, one in each regime of flow. However, for given U, D and d, there is only one slope.

Two different approaches were used in obtaining predictors for resistance. In the first approach, the total resistance is split into grain resistance and form resistance and the two are added to get the total resistance. Shen, Engelund, and Alam and Kennedy followed this approach. Whereas Engelund (75) 1967 related U / u'_* to R'_b / d, and $\tau'_0 / \Delta\gamma_s\, d$ to $\tau_o / \Delta\gamma_s\, d$ and regimes of flow, Alam and Kennedy (3) 1969 related grain friction factor f' to R_e and R_b/d and form friction factor f'' to R_b/d and $U / \sqrt{gd}$. It may be mentioned that by both these methods the prediction of U for known R, d and S is by trial and error process. Alternatively, the total resistance offered to the flow can be predicted using either a power type relation or logarithmic relation and parameters involved in them related to flow conditions. Equations proposed by Japanese engineers use the logarithmic relationship,

$$\frac{U}{u_*} = 5.75 \log \frac{R}{K_s} + 6.25 \tag{58}$$

where K_s/d was found to depend on $\tau_0 / (\gamma_s - \gamma_f)\, d$. However, the prediction of mean velocity by such formulation is found to be not very satisfactory. Liu and Hwang (189) 1961 proposed the following equation

$$U = C_a R^x S^y \tag{59}$$

where C_a, x and y are the functions of d and the regime of flow. However, this equation was based primarily on flume data and using it with field data has not met with great success. Garde and Ranga Raju (93) have shown that for all regimes of flow a single relationship exists, viz.

$$U \Big/ \sqrt{\frac{\Delta\gamma_s}{\rho_f} R} = f\left(\left(\frac{R}{d}\right)^{1/3} \frac{S}{\Delta\gamma_s/\gamma_f}\right)$$

Ranga Raju made modification in this by plotting

$K_1 U \Big/ \sqrt{\frac{\Delta\gamma_s}{\rho_f} R}$ vs $K_2 \left(\frac{R}{d}\right)^{1/3} \frac{S}{\Delta\gamma_s/\gamma_f}$ and related K_1 and K_2 to d.

Paris, Brownlie and others have similarly proposed other methods of predicting U. However, verification with large volume of data indicated that it was difficult to predict mean velocity U with less than ± 30 per cent error.

John F. Kennedy
(1933-1991)

John F. Kennedy (1933-1991) was born in Farmington, N. Mexico (USA) in 1933 and was educated at the University of Notre Dame and California Institute of Technology, (USA) from where he received B.S. and M.S., and Ph.D. respectively. Between 1961 and 1966 he worked as faculty member in the Civil Engineering Department of Massachusetts Institute of Technology, Cambridge (Mass.) USA. From 1966 till his premature death in December 1991, he was professor in the University of Iowa and Director of the Iowa Institute of Hydraulic Research.

In the field of Fluvial Hydraulics, Kennedy contributed significantly in the understanding of the mechanics of dune and antidune formation in erodible channels, resistance to flow, meander formation, sediment suspension in pipes, sediment transport, resistance, numerical modelling and scour prevention. While discussing the dune and antidune formation he introduced the concept of lag distance. In the area of resistance of flat bed in mobile bed channels, Lovera and Kennedy related f' not only to Re but R_b/d – a major departure from resistance analysis for rigid bed channels. He also radically departed from the conventional practice of independent analysis of resistance and sediment transport in steady uniform flows by relating

$$q_T/\gamma_s \sqrt{\Delta\gamma_s d^3/\rho_f}, \; R_b/d, \; U/\sqrt{\Delta\gamma_s d/\rho_f} \text{ and } (u_* - u_{*c})/\sqrt{\Delta\gamma_s d/\rho_f}$$

A computer code called IALLUVIAL was also developed in Iowa for computing transients in alluvial streams. Under Kennedy's guidance impetus was given to the study of ice problems. During his twenty five years at Iowa, Kennedy actively participated in IAHR activities and helped in the International efforts in Fluvial Hydraulic Research and Training.

Another significant contribution made by Odgaard and Kennedy is the development of Iowa Vanes.They have shown theoretically and by physical model (216) that short submerged vanes, installed at the incidence to the channel axis in the outer half of the river bend channel, significantly reduce the secondary currents and attendant undermining and high velocity attack on the outer bank.They have developed a design relationship for vane spacing which is a function of bend radius to channel width ratio, friction factor, exponent of velocity distribution law, height of vane to depth ratio, and vane angle with the axis.

It will be more appropriate to mention here the contribution to Fluvial Hydraulics of three other engineers.

Walter Hans Graf
(1936-)

Walter Hans Graf was born in Baden (Austria) in 1936; he received the diploma Ingg. from the University of Wien (Austria) in 1959 and Ph.D. from the University of California at Berkeley (USA) in 1963. Between 1963 and 1973 he worked in Cornell University, Ithaca, and Lehigh University, Bethelhem both in the USA and then moved to Laboratoire de Recherches Hydralique in Ecole Polytechnique Federale de Lausanne (Switzerland), as its director. Graf is known for his book titled "Hydraulics of Sediment Transport" first published in 1971. He has also authored books on Hydrodynamics, and Fluvial Hydraulics in French. Graf has worked on a variety of problems related to sediment transport in rivers and conduits, which include reservoir sedimentation, bed forms and resistance, bed-load transport at low shear values (226), sediment transport through pipes, and measurement of two phase flow in pipes (110), effect of unsteadiness of flow in the transport of sediment, effect of turbulence on the drag coefficient of immersed bodies and their fall velocity, flow in steep mobile bed channels, and boundary layer over permeable and impermeable rough surfaces. In this work, E.R. Acaroglu, G.C. Pazis, J.L. Boillat. O. Yucel, S.C. Ko and other were his associates.

M.S. Yalin's major contribution has been in developing a method for prediction of dune steepness as a function of $u_* d/\nu$, d/D, and τ_0/τ_{oc} (294) 1979. On the basis of plotting recently collected additional data on the incipient motion of nearly uniform sized material, Yalin and Karahan (295) 1979 have also modified Shields' curve for the incipient motion, which is now widely used. Other contributions of Yalin are related to river bed degradation, formation and modelling of dunes and meanders, physical modelling of flow in alluvial streams, probabilistic approach to saltation and suspension, flow resistance, and bed-load transport. Yalin's book on Sediment Transport was published a year later than that of Graf. Recently Yalin has also written a book on River Mechanics.

Arved Jaan Raudkivi
(1920–)

Arved Jaan Raudkivi was born in 1920 in Tallinn (Estonia) and completed his schooling there. He secured the first engineering degree, Diplma Ingenieur,in 1949 from the Technical University of Braunschweig (Germany), Ph.D. in Engineering from the University of Auckland (New Zealand), and Dr. Ing. in 1982 from the Technical University of Braunschweig. He worked for about eight years in Europe and New Zealand in the areas of harbours, structural engineering and hydro-power, and then joined the University of Auckland as lecturer in 1956. Since 1965 he worked as professor and retired in 1986. During his stay in the university as well as after retirement he has been working as active consultant in coastal engineering, water resources and fluvial hydraulics.

In the area of Fluvial Hydraulics, Raudkivi has worked on ripple formation and has measured the mean shear stress and turbulence along the ripple form. For predicting the channel resistance he suggested a graph between $\tau_0 / (\gamma_s - \gamma_f)\, d$ and $U / \sqrt{(u_*^2 - u_{*c}^2)}$, which showed different trends for the fine sands, sands and gravels. Other aspects studied by him include entrainment of granular particles by turbulent flow, erosion of cohesive soils, scour arounnd bridge piers, armouring, bed-forms, and bed-load transport in rivers and by waves (233). He is the author of books/monographs on Loose Boundary Hydraulics, Advanced Fluid Mechanics, Hydrology, and IAHR monographs on Scour and Sedimentation. His book on Loose Boundary Hydraulics covers well the contributions of Bagnold to sediment transport in rivers and under waves.

STABLE CHANNELS

During this period, some attempts were made to refine and generalise the regime theory using additional data, analyse channel shapes under no motion and sediment motion conditions, and synthesise the regime approach and sediment transport approach. Also the optimisation techniques were applied to stable channel adjustment problem.

Central Board of Irrigation and Power (India) collected data on many irrigation canals in India upto a discharge of about 300 m^3/s. In the USA, Simons and Bender collected data on 24 canals in the midwestern part of country and analysed these data along with other available data. In Pakistan, under a joint collaborative project betwee the USA and Pakistan, valuable data were collected under the project Canal Headworks Operation Programme (CHOP).

Fan (81) 1947, Glover and Florey (108) 1951, and Lane, Lin and Liu (177) 1959, obtained the cross-sectional profile of a channel under incipient motion condition. It can be expressed by the equation

$$D/D_{max} = \cos\left(\frac{x}{D_{max}} \tan\phi\right) \tag{60}$$

In the case of sediment transporting channels, Simons and Albertson (253) 1961 thought it necessary to classify channels into those with (i) sandy bed and banks, (ii) sandy bed and cohesive banks, (iii) cohesive bed and banks, and (iv) coarse non-cohesive materials. Essentially, for each one of the above types of channels they developed equations of the form

$$\left.\begin{aligned} &P,\ A,\ R = mQ^n \\ &U = \text{const.}\ (R^2 S)^P \\ \text{and}\quad &U^2/gDS = \text{const.}\ (UW/\nu)^{0.37} \end{aligned}\right\} \tag{61}$$

where m, n, p and the constants depend on the channel type. Chitale (44) 1966, proposed similar relationships. Gupta (114) 1967, and Kondap (165) 1977, used dimensional analysis and obtained equations of the type,

$$\frac{W_s}{d},\ \frac{A}{d^2},\ S = f\left(Q/d^2\ \sqrt{\Delta\gamma_s\, d/\rho_f},\ \overline{C}_T,\ g^{1/2}\, d^{3/2}/\nu\right)$$

They found that for the available data, sediment concentration had no effect on A, W_s and S of the channels.

Several attempts were made to include sediment load as one of the parameters in channel design; Lane (172) had stressed its importance. Inglis had found that Lacey's silt factors computed

$$f_1\,(U, R) = 2.52\ U^2/R$$

$$f_1\,(R, S) = 291\ R^{1/3}\ S^{2/3}$$

$$f_2\,(R, S, U) = 3127\ RS/U$$

are not equal. Applying Einstein's method of sediment load computation Ning Chien (210) 1957, showed that

$$\left.\begin{aligned} f_1\ (U, R) &= 0.061\ (q_T/q)^{0.715} \\ f_1\ (R, S) &= 2.2\, d^{0.45}\ (q_T/q)^{0.052} \end{aligned}\right\} \tag{62}$$

thus confirming f_1 (R, S) to be dependent primarily on sediment size. The weakest link in channel design has been the width equation.

Engelund and Hansen (75) 1967, used an empirical resistance law

$$U = 1951 d^{-3/4} D^{5/4} S^{9/8},$$

the sediment transport equation they had developed earlier, and the following empirical equation for the width

$$W = 6.97\, Q^{0.525} / d^{0.316} \qquad (62)$$

and prepared a design chart for obtaining *D*, *S* and *W* for a canal with known values of *Q*, *d* and Q_T. Here *d* is in mm.

Another approach to the channel design that has been explored during this time is the use of optimisation principle, which was attempted by Bharat Singh (25) 1964, Brebner and Wilson (30) 1967, Yang (297) 1974, Chang (41) 1980, Ramete (232) 1980, and White et al. (288) 1981. According to these studies (i) for a given *Q*, *d* and *S* the channel width and depth adjust in such a manner that Q_T is maximised, and (ii) for given *Q*, Q_T, and *d* the channel adjusts its width and depth in such a manner that *S* is minimised. White et al. (288) have shown that the two optimisations yield the same result. Chang (41) has given an algorithm to design a channel for known *Q*, Q_T, *d*, the side slope *Z* and water temperature. Two limitations of the optimisation approach have been pointed out. The first is that cohesivity of bank material plays an important role in restricting the width which is not considered here. Secondly even though optimisation seems to be a valid explanation, it cannot be used as a design method because exact amount of sediment load the channel would carry is not usually known.

Deryl B. Simons
(1918-)

Deryl B. Simons (1918-) received B.S. and M.S. from the Utah State University, Logan (USA) and worked from 1948 to 1957 in the University of Wyoming, Larami (USA) on a teaching assignment. From 1957 to 1963, he worked at the Colorado State University as USGS Research Chief and Hydraulic Engineer during which time he received his doctorate degree; his thesis was in the field of stable channels. He was also in charge of a project in which extensive data were collected on bed forms, resistance and sediment transport in laboratory flumes using sediments of various sizes. From 1965 to 1983 he worked in the Colorado State University in the capacity of professor, associate dean and director of engineering research centre. He has published profusely and has been an active consultant in the areas of Fluvial Hydraulics and river mechanics in USA and abroad. His major contributions in Fluvial Hydraulics have been in the areas of stable channels, flow regimes, effect of fine sediment on flow, resistance to flow, sediment transport, numerical modelling of transient flows, and river stabilisation.

E.V. Richardson was closely associated with the U.S. Geological Survey project on resistance and sediment transport at Colorado State University, Fort Collins (USA) between about 1956-1961, and later he joined the faculty of Civil Engineering there. Presently he is working as professor. D.B. Simons and E.V. Richardson worked closely for over twenty years on a number of research projects related to bed forms, resistance to flow, and stage-discharge curves in alluvial streams, bed-load and bed material transport, non-equilibrium river form, stochastic and mathematical modelling, effect of high concentration of fine material, sediment exclusion and ejection from canals, and design of spurs.

In the USA, the United States Geological Survey has been engaged in collecting data on sediment transport, resistance and plan forms on several streams in the USA. The data on rivers such as the Niobrara, Rio Puerco, East Fork, Middle Loup that have been collected under USGS programmes have been used by several investigators in the studies of fluvial hydraulics. B.R. Colby, C.F. Nordin, D.W. Hubbell, D.W. Dawdy and many other USGS scientists have published on above mentioned aspects. Hubbell's report (132) on the apparatus and technique of measurement of bed-load is an important USGS publication on bed-load measurement. W.W. Sayre who was for some time working in the Iowa Institute of Hydraulic Research and then in USGS has done work in the areas of channel resistance, and transport and dispersion of material in streams and channels.

LOCAL-SCOUR

Local scour around bridge piers and spurs, scour due to jets and downstream of hydraulic structures attracted the attention of engineers in this period. A large number of experiments were conducted by several investigators and some valuable data on scour around bridges were collected from the field. These investigators includes. Inglis, Laursen, Liu and Skinner, Garde et al., Sarma, Ishihara, Tison, Shen et al., Hjorth, Jain, Breussers, Hancu, Neill, Ettema and others. In India, the Research, Designs and Standards Organisation (RDSO) of Indian Railways has collected data on nine railway bridges. It was realised that scour needs to be studies under two categories, viz. clear water scour and scour under sediment transporting flow. One gets maximum scour under clear water condition; under sediment transporting flow, the equilibrium scour depth is somewhat smaller. Effect of opening ratio, pier shape, sediment size and flow condition on scour was studied. Some investigators found that scour is directly related to Froude number of the flow. Later, a model to compute time variation of scour and maximum scour has been developed by Kothyari (100). This includes consideration of stratification of the bed and sediment non-uniformity. Earlier these effects were also studied by

Ettema. In the case of scour due to jets, relative scour depth d_s/D_2 was found to be function of $q/H\omega_0$ and H/D where d_s is the scour below original bed level, D_2 is the downstream water depth, H is the height of fall and q is the discharge per unit width of two dimensional jet. However, most of the scour studies were carried out with uniform or near uniform materials and hence effect of armouring on scour was not studied. E. Partheniades who worked for some time at M.I.T. and then at the University of Florida has worked on erosion and deposition of cohesive soils and its stabilization.

TRANSIENT FLOWS

Availability of high speed computers to the academic staff since about 1960 gave a great impetus to the solution of problems related to the bed level variation in alluvial streams. Newton (208) 1951, conducted some laboratory experiments using uniform sediment and studied degradation. Lane (176) 1955, had classified the problems caused by disturbing a stream in equilibrium by increase and/or decrease of water or sediment discharge, change of water surface slope, and change in base level. This focussed attention on problems related to aggradation or degradation. Iwagaki (144) 1956, applied the method of characteristics to study the river bed variation. de Vries also studied this problem at Delft. Tinney (269) 1962, combined Manning's and du Boys equations with the continuity equation for sediment and obtained an expression for $\partial Z/\partial t$. Knowing the initial bed and water surface and upstream condition on Q_T (i.e. $Q_T = 0$ in case of clear water degradation) and downstream flow condition, a procedure was suggested to compute bed level at the end of tine ΔT. M. de Vries, J.A. Cunge, W.A. Thomas and others laid the foundation for developing computer codes for computations of bed and water surface in transient flows. Initially programmes were developed for one dimensional flow with quasi steady flow condition, i.e. when $\frac{\partial U}{\partial t}$ and $\frac{\partial D}{\partial t}$ were neglected, even in unsteady flows. The armouring effect was either neglected or accounted for empirically. Even though lag effect on bed-load transport was partially known the sediment transport law developed for steady uniform flow was used for unsteady non-uniform flows by replacing S_o by S_f. HEC-6 code developed by W.A. Thomas in USA in 1977, CHAR-2 developed by J.A. Cunge, France, CHAR-3 developed by J.A. Cunge and N. Perdeau, France in 1971; FLUVIAL II developed by H.H. Chang and R.D. Hill in the USA in 1976, SEDIMENT II developed by R. Ariathurai in 1976 and IALLUVIAL developed by Karim, Holly and Kennedy are a few such computer codes.

Simultaneously, laboratory experiments were conducted on armouring by Garde and Hasan (94) 1967, Gessler (104, 105), Little and Meyer (188) 1972, Davies (53) 1974, and Garde et al. (95) 1977, to know the mechanism of armouring and its prediction. Similarly, laboratory experiments on degradation were carried out by Shen et al. and Ilo (138) 1976. Laboratory experiments on aggradation upstream of a dam were conducted by Sugio (260) 1962, and Swamee and Garde

(262) 1977. Such studies provided an insight into the problem and in some cases some basic inputs in the formulation of computer codes. Similarly, field observations on the aggradation and degradation were carried out by Sonderegger (255) 1935, Hathaway (120) 1948, Bondurant (28) 1950, Vetter (282) 1953 and others. In the opinion of the author this analysis of transient flows is by far the most important contribution of this period to Fluvial Hydraulics which continued later with even greater vigour.

It will be in order to say a few words about Alexandre Preissmann, a mathematician, whose contributions to the computational hydraulics are greatly valued by those working in numerical modelling of transient flows in rivers and alluvial streams. The following information about him is extracted from the excellent introductory chapter written by M.B. Abbott and J.A. Cunge in the book on Computational Hydraulics (1). Preissmann graduated in mathematics from the Federal Institute of Technology in Zurich (Switzerland) and obtained the doctorate from the same institute in 1942. After working for an insurance company for four years, he joined his alma mater in the department of hydraulics and soil mechanics. Working under Meyer Peter, he studied various aspects of traditional and computational hydraulics e.g. water hammer, surge tanks, scale models, hydrology, sediment transport etc. Thus he became a mathematician and an engineer. As mentioned by Cunge, he was non-conformist, attaching little importance to material details and a lot to the intellectual life.

He joined SOGREAH (Societe Grenobloise d'Etudes et d'Applications Hydrauliques) at Grenoble (France) in 1958 and was responsible for the development of mathematical model for flood propagation, and was involved in one way or other in most of the mathematical modelling done there e.g. mathematical model of English Channel, tide propagation model, discharge regulation in Irrigation channels, vibration of antenae, CAREDAS (model for looped sewerage networks), and CARIMA (model for river networks).

It is not possible to go through all the contributions of Preissmann here; however it may be mentioned that several new ideas and schemes introduced by him, such as Preissmann scheme, Preissmann-Holly scheme, Preissmann pseudo-viscosity,and the Preissmann slot, have greatly helped in solving numerical difficulties, increasing the stability and accuracy of numerical schemes and in explaining the physical basis for successful numerical techniques. Preissmann retired in 1982 and expired recently. Preissmann has left a strong influence on his colleages and students who worked with him in SOGREAH, and on compuational hydraulics.

RESERVOIR SEDIMENTATION

Impetus to research on reservoir sedimentation was given by Brown (33) 1943. Then in India, Khosla (161) 1953, analysed the data from small and large reservoirs in India and abroad and obtained an empirical relationship between annual sediment yield V_s and catchment area A in the form $V_s = 3.23 \times 10^{-3} A^{0.72}$, where V_s is in Mm^3 and A in km^2 . Since only part of the sediment coming into the reservoir gets deposited there, one must know the trap efficiency. Brune (34) 1953, analysed the data from 44 normally ponded reservoirs in USA and developed a curve for trap efficiency as a function of capacity/inflow ratio. For the capacity/inflow ratio exceeding unity the trap efficiency was almost one hundred percent. Even after 40 years Brune's curve is still the best one available for the determination of trap efficiency. Borland and Miller (29) 1958 studied the distribution of sediment in reservoirs in the USA and proposed various empirical methods to determine the distribution of sediment at different elevations. In USA a large volume of data was collected from the reservoirs to determine the initial unit weights of deposited sediments and their compaction rates (164) 1958. Since about 1965 several large reservoirs in India are being monitored and valuable data are being collected about reservoir sedimentation. Bruk (35) 1985 has compiled a monograph in which methods of computing sedimentation in lakes and reservoirs have been discussed. The monograph deals with technical and economic impact of reservoir sedimentation, physical processes of sedimentation in reservoirs, field measurements, methods of preserving reservoir capacity and prediction methods. Chapter VI written in Bruk's monograph by Fan Jiahua from China discusses various methods used in China and other countries to regain the lost capacity of reservoirs.

FLOW IN BENDS AND MEANDERING

Flow in river bends received particular attention since that formed the basis for understanding the mechanics of meander formation. Rozovskii (235) 1957, studied the velocity distribution, resistance to flow, and generation and decay of secondary circulation in a wide rigid bend. Ippen and Drikner (140) 1962 measured the shear distribution on the bed of rigid bottom bends of various r/B and θ values in case of trapezoidal channels. Varshney (278) 1973, experimentally studied the scour profiles in rectangular bends with rigid side and erodible bed. Theoretical work on lateral bed profiles in channel bends has been carried out by Engleund (76) 1974, Kikkawa *et al.* (162) 1976, Zimmerman and Kennedy (302) 1978, and Odgaard.

The stability analysis has been used by many investigators to determine the conditions under which streams would meander. To carry out such an analysis one starts with the equations of motion and the continuity equations for sediment and water. Depending on whether the analysis is one, two or three dimensional, one, two or all the three equations of motion are utilised. One dimensional analysis was carried out by Voinieh-Syanozhenstki and Kereselidze (285) 1975, while two dimensional analysis has been carried out by Hansen (116) 1967, Callander (37) 1969, Parker (220) 1976, and Hayashi and Ozaki (123) 1978. Three dimensional analysis has been conducted by Engelund and Skovgaard (77) 1973, Hyashi (122) 1973, and Gottlieb (109) 1976. Such analysis differed depending on whether one used bed-load equation or total load equation in the analysis, on which resistance law is used, the nature of disturbance imposed, and on the degree of linearisation.

The analysis yields the conditions under which plan form would change to meandering or braiding. Such studies have indicated the importance of Froude number, BS/D, τ_*, D/B and u_*/u_{*c} as the important parameters.

It may be appropriate to make a mention of contribution of Tiazo Hayashi from the Chuo University Tokyo (Japan) who was born at Nagoya (Japan) in 1920 and received his bachelor's and doctoral degrees from the Tokyo Imperial University and Tokyo Universty respectively. After working in these universities between 1942 and 1949 he joined the Chuo University in 1950 and has been the professor since 1954 to date. He has done excellent work on the critical tractive stress of non-uniform materials, saltation of sediment particles, sediment transport of mixtures, stability analysis to explain formation of dunes and antidunes, bed-form analysis, meander formation and resistance to flow. He has also carried out analysis of flood waves, forces on break waters by the action of breaking waves, and diffusion of warm water surface jet.

Tiazo Hayashi
(1920-)

T. Tsujimoto who was earlier working at the Disaster Prevention Research Institute, Kyoto and then moved to the Kanagawa University has also made significant contributions to lag behaviour of unsteady flow with dunes, stochastic study of saltation, longitudinal sorting, scour around structures and sediment transport under unsteady non-uniform flow conditions. In fact a large number of scientists are very active in many Japanese Universities and research institutes and studying problems related to Fluvial Hydraulics. China-Japan workshop held in 1984 lists a large number of papers published by Japanese engineers either in Japanese or in English on various aspects of Fluvial Hydraulics. Others who have made notable contributions are K. Ashida, A. Daido, A. Furuya, T. Kishi, T. Ishihara, T. Itakura, T. Tsubaki, H. Kikkawa, M. Kurihara, S. Tanaka and T. Tsuchiya.

PROBABILISTIC AND STOCHASTIC APPROACHES

It may be recalled that earlier Einstein and then Kalinske used some probabilistic concepts in the theory of bed-load movement. The period under consideration saw increasing use of this approach to sediment movement and channel hydraulics. Hubbell and Sayre (133) 1964, and Sayre and Hubbell (245) 1965, presented one dimensional stochastic model for the transport of bed material particles in alluvial channel, in which transport of a particle is described as an alternating sequence of step lengths and rest periods. Yang, and Griggs experimentally determined the step length which followed closely the gamma distribution and the rest period which followed exponential law. Nordin (214) 1971, treated bed level variation in an undulated bed as a stochastic process and studied the statistical properties of the dune profile. In 1971, the first symposium on Stochastic Hydraulics was held at the University of Pittsburgh, Penn. (USA) where some papers were published on stochastic modelling of sediment transport phenomena.

Jain and Kennedy (147) 1974 studied the spectral evolution of bed forms in an alluvial channel. In the plan form analysis, some investigators have proposed a random walk model to explain meandering. It is postulated that when a river travels a step length, it has three choices viz. it can travel straight, go to the left or go to the right. On the basis of this hypothesis, it was possible to obtain meander pattern.

MOVABLE BED MODELS

As mentioned earlier, the first movable bed model of the Garonne river near Bordeaux was built and tested by Fargue in 1875. The model was undistorted one with the length scale of 100. The time and velocity scales were, however, not properly defined. Since then physical movable bed models have been used to study various alluvial river problems in a large number of countries. Contributions of Reynolds and Froude in the latter part of 19th century clarified the roles of viscosity and gravity in hydraulic models. During the first quarter of this century German and some European laboratories were very busy in conducting sediment studies and model studies on rivers. These activities have been described by Freeman (85).

After Lacey published his work on regime theory, a new method for design of models of rivers with movable beds was given by Lacey, Inglis and then Blench, who used the regime equations for determining the scales of the model for known length (or discharge) scale and the scale of sediment size. With little modification this method is still used in India. From the consideration of dynamics of flow, it can be shown that τ_*, Fr and $u_* d/\nu$ must be kept the same in the model and prototype which is very difficult to attain in general. Garde and Ranga Raju (101) have shown that in the models based on Lacey's method, Froude number is maintained the same in the model and prototype only if sediment size scale d_r = 1.0. Further, to cause appreciable sediment movement at the dominant discharge, slope distortion has to be resorted to; i.e. $S_r = \eta\, h_r / L_r$ and $\eta = dr$. The distortion L_r/h_r is kept less than 6 or 7 and h_r lies between $L_r^{2/3}$ and $L_r^{3/4}$. With these guidelines the model is designed. Usually such model gives only qualitative prediction of the river behaviour and quantitative predictions cannot be done since similarity in sediment transport is not fully achieved.

Rational approach to the design of distorted river bed models has been proposed by Einstein (62, 69). However, the method proposed by him is too rigid in that if all the conditions specified by him are to be fulfilled, only one scale ratio can be freely chosen. For every relaxation of the condition an additional distortion is introduced. Using the frame work of sediment transport theory, a large number of investigators have proposed methods for scales determination and these methods have been used in their own laboratories, e.g. de Vries, Gehrig, Bogardi, Komura, Zwamborn and others. Considerable progress has also been made in China and this can be seen from the papers published in the proceedings of International Symposia on River Sedimentation.

One of the approaches which is more appealing and which seems to give reasonably good quantitative predictions is the method proposed by Zwamborn (303, 304). He advocates the equality of u_* / ω_0 in place of $\tau_0 / (\gamma_s - \gamma_f)\, d$ and $U_* \, d / \nu$. He further stipulates that $(u_* \, d / \nu)_r$ be less than proximately ten, and L_r/h_r less than four. With these conditions, equality of Fr and $C_r = S_r^{-1/2}$, it is possible to design the model, which gives good quantitative conformity between model and prototype. This method was used for designing models of the Notchwan and the Umfolozi rivers in South Africa and very good conformity between model of prototype results was obtained.

Aerodynamic models for studying the flow phenomena in streams have been used in the USSR since 1941. They are also used in several European countries such as Yugoslavia, Poland, Romania, Hungary, Germany, Portugal and France. These models are small in size and hence less expensive to operate. Hence they are best suited for preliminary studies.

It may be mentioned that with greater progress made in computer simulation and the increased cost of labour, relatively smaller emphasis is nowadays placed on physical models, even though for solving some three dimensional local problems, only physical model would provide a means to predict prototype behaviour.

CONTRIBUTIONS FROM INDIA

Since about 1960, systematic investigations are being conducted in the area of Fluvial Hydraulics at the University of Roorkee (India), through a series of M.E. and Ph.D theses. The subjects dealt with included mechanism of resistance to flow, regimes of flow and resistance, effect of pier size and shape, sediment size and flow conditions on scour, bed form movement, transport of uniform and non-uniform sediments, fine sediment transport and its effect on velocity distribution and resistance, stable channels, flow around bends, aggradation and degradation caused by withdrawal of clear water, addition of clear water and decrease or increase of sediment load, sedimentation of reservoirs, erosion from catchments, and armouring. The major emphasis has been on collection of data

K.G. Ranga Raju
(1942-)

in the laboratory, and use of all available data from field and laboratory studies for drawing generalised conclusions. To share the knowledge, International Workshops on Alluvial River Problems are held by the University of Roorkee at intervals of about four years; the first such workshop was held in 1980 and then in 1985 and 1989. These studies at Roorkee were carried out under the direction of the author and K.G. Ranga Raju.

Born in 1942 at Bangalore (India), K.G. Ranga Raju obtained Bachelor's degree in Civil Engineering from the University of Bangalore, and came to Roorkee to complete M.E. and Ph.D. in Hydraulic Engineering. Since 1963 he is on the faculty of Civil Engineering Department of Roorkee University and is working as Professor since 1975.

He has been closely associated with the author in most of the research in Fluvial Hydraulics carried out at Roorkee University since 1963 or so, on regimes of flow, resistance, sediment transport of uniform and non-uniform materials, scour, dispersion, aggradation and degradation. In addition, he has also worked on flow measurement using weirs, developing boundary layers, and hydraulic structures.

Mention may also be made of the contributions made by Srikrishna Vishnu Chitale who was working at the Central Water and Power Research Station, Khadkwasla (India).

Chitale was born in 1920 and had his all the technical degrees from the University of Poona. Working in C.W. and P.R.S. Pune for thirty four years he retired in 1978 as Joint Director. Chitale's major contributions have been in the analysis of river and stable channel data, and developing statistical formulae for the geometrical and hydraulic parameters for rivers and channels. He has also studied plan forms and meandering of the rivers, and made recommendations on the waterways for the bridges, geometry and dimensions of the guide bunds, and sediment excluders. In addition, he has worked on a variety of specific applied problems related to river control that were referred to C.W. and P.R.S. He has authored or co-authored books on Stable Channels, Design Practices of Irrigation Canals, Stream Gauging, River Behaviour, Control and Training, and River Training and Bank Protection Works for Railway Bridges.

S.V. Chitale
(1920-)

The research stations at Khadakwasla, Roorkee and Amritsar in India have also conducted several studies and evolved designs of sediment excluding devices and specific river training measures for many river valley projects in India.

DISSEMINATION OF INFORMATION

During this period major effort was made to make the information on Fluvial Hydraulics available to engineers and students. This was accomplished through holding conferences, publishing annotated bibliographies, publishing articles in Journals and publishing books.

In many universities a graduate course in Erosion and Sedimentation was offered, and gradually some essential parts of the subject percolated to undergraduate curriculum. Several research papers were presented in the biennial congresses of IAHR, speciality conferences of ASCE and other societies. A separate subcommittee was formed by IAHR to look after advancement in Fluvial Hydraulics. A.S.C.E. started the Journal of Hydraulics Division which contained many articles in Fluvial Hydraulics. After 1948, Federal Interagency Conferences in the USA were exclusively devoted to the sediment problems. In India, Central Board of Irrigation and Power held annual research sessions in which problems related to rivers, stable channels, and sediment exclusion wer discussed.

In addition, the Transactions of American Geophysical Union (USA), Water Resources Research Journal of AGU, Journal of Sedimentology, Journal of Hydrology of Netherlands, La Houille Blanche from France, and Journals of the Institution of Civil Engineers from UK and other countries contained many papers on Fluvial Hydraulics.

In the USA, the Subcommittee on Hydrology of the Federal Interagency River Basin Committee prepared an annotated bibliography on Hydrology in 1952 for the period 1941-1950, and in 1955, they published annotated bibliography on Hydrology and Sedimentation. Later similar bibliographies on Hydrology and Sedimentation were prepared and published periodically by the U.S. Geological Survey.

A large number of books were written on Fluvial Hydraulics and Sedimentation during this period. In 1950, C.B. Brown wrote a chapter on Sediment Transport in Engineering Hydraulics edited by H. Rouse. It covered discussion on sediment properties, sediment transport, reservoir sedimentation, and sediment exclusion.

United Nations published reports on River Training and Bank Protection, and on Sediment Problem in 1952 and 1955 respectively. Serge Leliavsky wrote a book on Introduction to Fluvial Hydraulics in 1955. This books gives short but excellent survey of the earlier developments in this field. In Japan, Yuichi Iwagaki wrote a comprehensive chapter on Sediment Transport in the Applied Hydraulics Treatise edited by T. Ishihara in 1956. Some other books published during this period are listed below:

1. Manual of River Behaviour, Control and Training. CBIP, India, Publ. No. 60, 1956.

2. Rozovski, I.L. Flow of Water in Bends of Open Channels. Academy of Sciences of Ukranian SSR, 1957.
3. Kondratev, N E. (Ed.). River Flow and River Channel Formation. 1959.
4. Razanitsyn, N. A. Morphological and Hydrological Regularities of the Structures of the River Net. 1960.
5. Vanoni, V.A., N.H. Brooks, and J.F. Kennedy. Lecture Notes on Sediment Transportation and Channel Stability. Caltec. Rep. No. KH-R-1, 1961.
6. Goncharov V.N. Dynamics of Channel Flow. Israel Programme of Scientific Translation, 1962.
7. Einstein H.A., Chapter on "River Sedimentation" in Handbook on Applied Hydrology. McGraw Hill Book Co. N.Y. 1964.
8. Leopold, L.B., M.G. Wolman and J.P. Miller. Fluvial Processes in Geomorphology. Freeman and Company, USA, 1964.
9. Chitale, S.V. Hydraulics of Stable Channels. Manager of Publications, Govt. of India, 1966.
10. Raudkivi A.J. Loose Boundary Hydraulics. Pergamon Press, UK, 1967.
11. Morisawa, M. Streams: Their Dynamics and Morphology. Earth Science Series, McGraw Hill Book Co. N.Y. 1968.
12. Chorley, R.J. (Ed.), Water, Earth and Man. Methuen, London, 1969.
13. Shen H.W. (Ed). River Mechanics. W.R. Publication, USA Vol. I and II. 1971.
14. Graf, W.H. Hydraulics of Sediment Transport. McGraw Hill Book Co. N.Y., 1971.
15. Bogardi, J. Sediment Transport in Alluvial Streams. Hungarian Academy of Sciences, Budapest, 1971. (Translated in English in 1978).
16. Yalin, M.S. Mechanics of Sediment Transport. Pergamon Press Ltd. Oxford, UK, 1972.
17. Vanoni, V.A. (Ed.), Sedimentation Engineering. A.S.C.E., 1975.
18. Garde R.J. and K.G. Ranga Raju. Mechanics of Sediment Transportation and Alluvial Stream Problems. Wiley Eastern Ltd. Publishers, New Delhi, 1977.
19. Simons, D.B. and F. Sentürk. Sediment Transport Technology. Water Resources Publicatons, Littleton, Colo. (USA), 1977.

CONCLUDING REMARKS

It can thus be seen that during 1950-1975 significant advance was made in Fluvial Hydraulics. Using a large volume of laboratory and field data various approaches were made for prediction of resistance and sediment transport rates. There was greater effort in developing mathematical models and developing computer codes for calculations of bed level variation in transient flows. Further, stability analysis and optimisation methods were used to analyse problems of bed forms, plan forms, and hydraulic geometry of channels. Lastly, a much larger number of scientists from different countries participated and contributed to the development of Fluvial Hydraulics.

Chapter 8

Developments Since 1975

The pace of the development of Fluvial Hydraulics which picked up during 1950-1975 continued after 1975 with even greater vigour. This was characterised by a greater international participation in the research efforts, closer cooperation between researchers from different countries, and greater emphasis on numerical modelling. The number of publications which came out in Fluvial Hydraulics during this period is so large that it is not possible to do justice to all of them in such a publication of historical nature. The second reason for this inability fact that their full implication as well as their limitations have not yet been fully established.

SOIL EROSION

Even though research on soil erosion was started earlier, it received impetus since the middle of the century and greater progress was achieved during the period under consideration. One may get the idea about the seriousness of soil erosion problem from the fact that it has been estimated that about 20-40 billion tons of soil is taken to the sea annually through the rivers due to natural erosion, intensive agriculture, grazing and other construction activities. Realising the serious implications of the accelerated erosion on agricultural productivity and the environment, efforts are made to collect the data by carrying out laboratory and field studies, to understand the mechanics of soil erosion and to develop predictive models.

Erosion rates from different catchments vary over a very wide range; whereas the minimum erosion rates observed are 1-2 tons/km^2/year, very high values of the order of 10,000 to 30,000 tons/km^2/year have been obtained from some catchments in China, Taiwan, Java and New Zealand. To know the basic parameters which affect erosion, experiments have to be conducted under controlled conditions. Hence researchers have used rainfall simulators, which produce rainfall of known intensity, duration and raindrop size. Rainfall simulators are used in the laboratory as well as on field plots. A workshop on rainfall simulators was arranged in the USA in 1979 which provides information on rainfall simulators (272). With the advent of microprocessors, programmable rainfall simulators have been developed and used (83).

Some soil loss prediction models have been developed. The most commonly quoted equation for soil loss from agricultural areas is the Universal Soil Loss Equation — USLE which predicts the annual erosion rate from sheet and rill erosion (171); it was developed in USA. Similar equation known as SLEMSA (Soil Loss Estimator for South Africa) was developed in South Africa (72) in 1981. More comprehensive models include equations for detachment by raindrop impact, detachment by flow, transport by flow and deposition by flow. Using such equations a programme has been developed for studing erosion. One such model is known as CREAMS : A field scale model for Chemicals, Run off and Erosion for Agricultural Management Systems (273). This is used by soil conservation service in the USA. Lal (171) has discussed various research methods used in soil erosion. In the case of large catchments, models based on microanalysis become cumbersome. In such case one identifies macroparameters on which erosion from the catchment depends and using data from reservoir sedimentation studies, working relationships are developed. Such an attempt for Indian catchments has been made by Garde and Kothyari (98) in which they related annual sediment yield to annual mean precipitation, drainage density, average catchment slope, vegetal cover factor and (P_{max}/p_a) where P_{max} is the average maximum monthly rainfall and P_a is the annual mean precipitation. In the United Kingdom D.E. Walling from the University of Exeter has done an excellent work on the collection and analysis of world wide data on erosion.

VELOCITY DISTRIBUTION

Song and Yang (256) 1979 have derived a velocity distributiuon law using the theory of minimum rate of energy expenditure. For turbulent flow in wide open channels they considered two distinct layers of flow within the boundary layer. The two layers were y/D less than 0.50 and y/D greater than 0 50. The inner layer had a logarithmic velocity distributiuon law while the outer layer had a parabolic law with constant eddy viscosity. The constants in the two equations were determined using the theory of minimum rate of energy expenditure. Their equations in the form of velocity defect law are

$$\left.\begin{aligned} \frac{(u_{max} - u)}{u_*} &= -\frac{1}{4\beta_1}\left(\ln\frac{2y}{D} - \frac{1}{2}\right) \text{ for } \frac{\delta'}{D} \le \frac{y}{D} \le 0.50 \\ \text{and} \qquad \frac{(u_{max} - u)}{u_*} &= \frac{(1 - y/D)^2}{2\beta_1} \text{ for } 0.50 \le \frac{y}{D} \le 1.0 \end{aligned}\right\} \qquad (64)$$

Here δ' is the thickness of laminar sublayer and $4\beta_1$ = Karman constant of 0.40. The above equation was derived for flat rigid bed; however they have shown that the equations are valid for mobile bed channels with small bed undulations. This needs verification. Itakura and Kishi (143) 1980, have derived a velocity distribution law for sediment laden flows using Monin-Obukhov length. They have proposed the equation

$$\left.\begin{aligned} (u - u_{max}) / u_* &= \frac{1}{\kappa}\left[\ln\frac{y}{D} + D_*\left(\frac{y}{D} - 1\right)\right] \\ \text{where} \quad D_* &= \frac{2.8\,\Delta\gamma_s \cdot D\,\omega_0\,\overline{C}_s}{\rho_f u_*^3} \end{aligned}\right\} \tag{65}$$

and $\kappa = 0.40$, and $\overline{C}_s$ is the average volumetric concentration of the suspended sediment. This distribution has been checked for flow in rigid bed channels and its application to alluvial bed with bed undulations remains to be studied.

Coleman (49) 1981, has proposed a velocity distribution equation for steady uniform turbulent flow with suspended sediment. It takes the form

$$\frac{(u_{max} - u)}{u_*} = -\frac{2.3}{\kappa}\log\frac{y}{\delta} + \frac{2\Pi}{\kappa} - \frac{\Pi}{\kappa} f\left(\frac{y}{\delta}\right) \tag{66}$$

Here δ is the thickness of boundary layer where maximum velocity occurs, and $\frac{\Pi}{\kappa} f(y/\delta)$ is the wake region velocity augmentation function, and Π is the wake strength coefficient.

$$f(y/\delta) = 2\sin^2\left(\frac{\Pi}{2}\frac{y}{\delta}\right) \tag{67}$$

and Π is related to gross Richardson number $R_i = \frac{g\delta\,(\rho_\delta - \rho_f)}{\rho_{mix}\,u_*^2}$. No method is given to determine ρ_δ and ρ_{mix}, and for their determination suspended load distribution must be known.

Lastly Samaga (243) 1984 has proposed a two layer model the two layers being $\frac{y}{D} \le 0.20$ and $\frac{y}{D} \ge 0.20$. The equations proposed are

$$\left.\begin{aligned} \frac{u}{u_*} &= 28.5\,\frac{y}{D}\left(1 - \frac{y}{2D}\right) + B \quad \text{for } d_a \le y \le 0.20\,D \\ \frac{u}{u_*} &= 5.75\log\frac{y}{d_a} + A \quad \text{for } y \ge d_a \end{aligned}\right\} \tag{68}$$

where A and B are increasing functions of D/d_a; "A" ranged from 5.1 to 9.0 and "B" ranged from 7.5 to 20 for D/d_a changing from 100 to 1800. This was primarily for flat bed. It was suggested that if u_* is replaced by u_*' the above equations will be valid for dune bed also; but this was not verified. In the above equation d_a is the arithmetic mean size of the bed material.

It can thus be seen that Coleman, and Itakura and Kishi have obtained velocity distributiuon laws which depend on the prior knowledge of suspended load concentration and its distribution.The other two distributions proposed by Song and Yang, and Samaga have been primarily developed for flat bed and need to be checked for bed with undulations. It is felt that velocity distribution in the lower layer in case of dune bed needs to be studied in greater detail.

SEDIMENT TRANSPORT

In the analysis of distribution of the suspended load in the vertical, the major concept introduced during this period was two layer distributions. This was done by Antsyferov and Kosyan (8) 1980, McTigue (198) 1981 and Samaga (243) 1984. Antsyferov and Kosyan indicated that Eq. 43 does not describe the concentration distribution in the vertical correctly if $\omega_0 > 0.27\, u_*$. They introduced an additive term for ε_s for $y/D < 0.20$ and have obtained a complicated equation for C/C_a which needs to be integrated numerically to get C. Similarly McTigue has suggested the equations

$$\left.\begin{aligned} C/C_a &= e^{-\omega_0 (y-a)/\kappa_1 u_* D} && \text{for } 0.20 \le \frac{y}{D} \le 1.0 \\ C/C_a &= \left(\frac{y}{a}\right)^{-\omega_0/\kappa_2 u_*} && \text{for } \frac{y}{D} \le 0.2 \end{aligned}\right\} \quad (69)$$

Here $\kappa_1 = 0.11$ and $\kappa_2 = 0.35$ were obtained from the analysis of experimental data. Samaga, took the reference concentration at C_a at $y/D = 0.20$ and proposed different values of Z in the equation

$$\frac{C}{C_a} = \left(\frac{D-y}{4y}\right)^Z \quad (70)$$

for upper and lower layers. The exponent Z for upper and lower layers Z_U and Z_L, and $C_{0.2D}$ were related to u'_*/ω_0 and $\frac{U/\omega_0}{\tau'_*}$. Itakura and Kishi (143) 1980 used the equation

$$C/C_a = \left[\left(\frac{D-y}{D-a}\right)^{1+D_*} \frac{a}{y}\right]^{Z_0} \quad (71)$$

and related C_a at $0.05D$ to parameter $\left(\frac{\rho_s - \rho_f}{\rho_f}\right)\frac{gd\,\Omega}{\omega_0\, u_*}$ where Ω is a function of τ_*. Wills in 1979 propsed a concentration distribution model using an error function for ε_s.

Two other aspects of sediment transport received attention during this period. First concerns the effect of sediment non-uniformity on transport. Earlier, most of the experiments on sediment transport were carried out on uniform or near uniform sediments with small standard deviation. The non-uniformity of sediment introduces two complications namely the hiding effect of small particles behind the coarser ones and exposure of coarser particles to higher velocity. After Einstein's work on this topic in 1950, very few data were collected and analysed. This has been done by Misri et al. (204) and Samaga (243) for bed-load and total load respectively. They collected fractionwise bed-load and total load data in laboratory flumes using bed materials with a wider range of median sizes and standard deviation. On the basis of these and other data they have proposed a method for computation of total load and its size distribution under steady uniform flow conditions. Similar studies have been conducted by Proffitt and Sutherland (228) also, who have modified Ackers and White, and Paintal's formulae to take into account sediment non-uniformity.

The second aspect concerns about the sediment transport under unsteady, non-uniform flow condition. In the earlier stage of development of mathematical models, the sediment transport law valid for steady uniform flow was used in unsteady non-uniform flow condition. Part of the discrepancies between calculated and observed bed elevations is attributed to this assumption. Hence attempts are made to develop a transport law under unsteady, non-uniform flow conditions. Under such conditions, the temporal and spatial derivatives of the flow parameters and the transport rate would become more complex. Further, after a sudden change of the flow parameter such as discharge, sediment transport becomes unsteady or non-uniform even for steady flow conditions, because of relaxation that is brought about by the fact that fluvial process, represented as a closely interrelating system, requires time to respond to the change of flow conditions. Empirical and semi-empirical equations have been proposed by many (11, 12, 21, 55, 213, 261, 271, 300). In this regard engineers from China and Japan have made significant contributions. The major difficulty in the development of sediment transport equation under unsteady non-uniform flow conditions is the non-availability of experimental data.

Other aspect of sediment transport which attracted the attention during this period is the transport of cohesive sediment. Physical processes constituting fine, cohesive sediment in esturine water are described. These processes include settling and deposition, consolidation, erosion and transport in suspension. Two excellent review papers published in Journal of Hydraulic Engineering of ASCE (201, 202) give the state of art in this respect.

Lastly, realising the fact that accuracy of prediction of bed profiles would to a great extent depend on the accuracy of resistance and sediment transport laws used, comparisons of resistance and sediment transport laws available were made using a set of field data. Such comparisons for prediction of the regimes of flow has been done by Garde and Anil Kumar (99) while for resistance and sediment transport, such comparisons have been made by Thompson (266) and Vetter (283).

MATHEMATICAL MODELS

One of the difficult problems in Fluvial Hydraulics is how to predict the surface layer composition of the degrading bed during the transient condition as well as in the final armoured stage. The experimental and analytical work related to solution of this problem has been carried out. Two types of degradation have been visualised. If the applied shear stress, in the case of non-uniform material, is less than the critical shear for d_{90} size of the bed material, parallel lowering of the bed would occur. If the applied shear stress is greater than the critical shear for d_{90}, initially rotational degradation would occur, thus reducing the applied shear and this is followed by parallel degradation. Conceptual models have been proposed to study variations of size distribution of surface layer in both the cases by Gessler (104), Bayazit (19), Shen and Liu (251), Karim and Holly (154), Lee and Odgaard (183) and Palaniappan (217).

In modelling aggradation and degradation, two approaches have been followed. Earlier de Vries had shown that for one dimensional motion under certain assumptions, equation of motion, continuity equations for sediment and water, sediment transport law and the resistance law can be combined and simplified to give either a parabolic or hyperbolic partial differential equation in Z, the bed elevation. These equations have been solved either analytically or numerically by Soni *et al.* (257), Mehta *et al.* (200), Jaramillo and Jain (148), Zhang Hou and Kahawita (300), Ribberink and Van der Sande, Gill, and Phillips and Sutherland. In this regard valuable experimental data on aggradation and degradation, caused by increase or decrease of water discharge or increase or decrease of sediment load, have been collected at the University of Roorkee in India by Soni, Mehta, and Yadav (291) and have been used in verification of mathematical models.

Another approach has been to develop computer programmes to solve complete set of equations. Garde *et al.* (97) and Palaniappan (217) have developed such models in India for aggradation and aggradation/degradation respectively, and applied to Gobindsagar reservoir and downstream of Milburn dam in the USA. Many such models have been developed all over the world and some of these have been listed in Table 3. In the numerical solution of the set of governing equations, significant contributions have been made by A. Preissmann, J.A. Cunge, M.B. Abbott, F.M. Holly, C.B. Vreugdenhil, M. de Vries, N. Perdeau, G.J. Klassen, B.G. Krishnappan and others (1).

Table 3: Some mathematical models developed since 1975 (55, 217)

Name	Author	Year	Description	
		One — Dimensional Models		
LPM	Soni et al., UOR	1980	SM	A
LHM	Mehta et al., UOR	1983	SM	A
LHM	Jarmamillo et al., Iowa	1984	SM	N and A
	Zhang Hou	1987	SM	N and A
NLHM	Ribberink	1987	SM	A
HEC 2 SR	Simons et al.	1980	QS	FD
FLUVIAL	Chang et al.	1976	QS	FD
IALLUVIAL	Karim et al.	1982	QS	FD

Name	Author	Year	Description	
YONG	Yong, Taiwan	1984	QS	FD
USGS	Bennet et al., USA	1983	US	FD
BOGNAR	Bognar et al., Hungary	1986	US	FD
SYSTEM II	Marno et al.	1989	US	FD
CARICHAR	Rahuel et al., France, USA, China	1988	US	CFD
1-D Math Model	Ashida, DPRI, Kyoto	1980		
1-D Math Model	State Geological Institute	1985		
M-1-NENU	Han Qiwei and He Minming, IWHR, China	1985		FD
1-D Math	Wang Shiqing et al., Tsinghua Univ., China	1991		FD
		2-Dimensional Models		
CHARIMA	F.M. Holly,	1988-1994	US	FD
		(General purpose computer code for steady or unsteady water, sediment and contaminant movement in simple, braided or looped networks).		
RIVCOH	Delft Hydraulic Laboratory			FD
RIVMOR-2D	Delft Hydraulic Laboratory			FD
2D Model	Hohai University, China, 1990			FD
2D Model	Wang Shangyi et al.	Tianjin University, China, 1990		FD
		Quasi 3-D and 3-D Mathematical Models		
SUSTRA	Delft Hydraulics Laboratory	1987		FD
QUASI 3-D	Wang and Adoff, USA	1986		FD

A — Analytical Solution, N — Numerical Methods, FD — Finite Difference Models, SM — Simplified Models, QS — Quasi Steady Model, US–Unsteady model, CFD–Coupled Finite Difference Model.

A few general comments can be made about the direction in which the progress is being made in mathematical modelling of alluvial streams. With the avilability of very powerful computers at reasonable costs, less consideration is now given to economies in the computer memory and in the computational efforts, and priority in programming techniques is given to reducing costs towards software use and in facilitating software maintenance (22). In the case of modelling the physical processes involved in bed level computations the following comments can be made. Fluid flow, sediment transport, particle sorting or bed material coarsening, and the bed level evolution are elements of a coupled process. However, they all have different time scales and changes in one aspect in a given time step may or may not induce significant changes in the others. Hence questions are raised about processes which should be coupled and those which should not be coupled.

There is considerable awareness that a real progress in modelling of the complex processes in river bed evolution can be made more efficiently when research and user organisations work together. Thus, the Iowa Institute of Hydraulic Research (IIHR), USA, Laboratoire d'Hydraulique de France (LHF), Grenoble, France, and the German Administration for Waterways (BAW – Bundesanstalt für Wasserbau), Germany, modified and consolidated the original SEDICOUP programme and used it for modelling Danube/Isar sedimentation problems.

Lastly, some of the recently developed computer codes include using complete Saint Venant's equations rather than making an assumption of quasi steady flow; computing the sediment load fractionwise, and as bed-load and suspended load separately; updating of friction factor; coupling of flow and sediment equations; adding energy loss at weirs, bridges and sills; considering sediment transport over rock outcrops and non-erodible reaches; and considering looped networks as in braided channels.

Some progress has also been made in the modelling of flow in bends and meandering phenomenon. Between 1984-1989 A.J. Odgaard has published several papers in the Journal of Hydraulic Engineering of ASCE on the modelling of river meanders. Writing equations of motion in curvilinear orthogonal system and introducing the velocity distribution in longitudinal and lateral directions caused due to centrifugal action, bank migration is studied using two models namely, (i) using Ikeda's hypothesis that rate of bank retreat or migration is proportional to and in phase with the difference between near-bank and section average velocities and (ii) the rate of bank retreat is related to increase in near-bank scour depth. Such models have also been proposed by G. Parker, H. Chang, Fredsoe, Hayashi, Engelund and others. However, the lithology of the terrain exerts such a strong influence on meander geometry that one wonders whether the plan form of the river can ever be fully predicted by such mathematical models.

Another area in which mathematical modelling is used is for explaining the formation of alternate bars and other meso bed forms in alluvial streams. This has been done by Hayashi and Ozaki, Ikeda, Kishi and Kuroki, and others. Such analysis normally lead to a criterion for plan forms such as between τ_* and BS/D, τ_* and B/D, Fr and u_*/u_{*c} and τ_* and Fr.

Still another area in which mathematical modelling is used is the performance of rectangular settling basins. Here equations of motion involving turbulence terms are used and using techniques of turbulence modelling of the correlation terms equations are solved, as indicated by Celik and Rodi (40).

GRAVEL-BED RIVERS

During the past 12 years a lot of interest has been evinced in understanding the hydraulics of gravel rivers in which it is only during the very high flows that most sizes of the bed material move and for lower discharges bed is paved with non-movable layer. Such rivers have been studied in UK, Canada and some other countries. The first International Conference on Gravel Bed Rivers (126) was held in UK in 1980 and since then these conferences have been held at regular intervals. The aspects of gravel bed rivers that are studied include resistance, cross-sectional geometry, sediment transport, bank erosion and stabilisation, plan forms, channel response, and regime analysis. It is worth noting that the geographers and geomorphologists from UK, Canada, USA and New Zealand have taken active interest in the analysis of gravel-bed rivers. Gary Parker, R.D. Hey, C.R. Thorne, J.C. Bathurst and J. Lewin are some of the scientists, who have made contributions to the flow in gravel rivers.

Gary Parker, who earlier studied in the University of Alberta (Canada), joined the St. Anthony Falls Hydraulic Laboratory of the University of Minnesota (USA) in the early 80's. His work in the area of Fluvial Hydraulics is related to the bar resistance of and transportation of bed-load in gravel-bed rivers, bed form analysis, cause and characteristics of meandering and braiding of streams, armouring and paving, and analysis of straight self formed streams (219, 220, 221, 222).

HYPER CONCENTRATION FLOWS

Some of the rivers in China carry very high sediment concentration of fine sediment. Many times the concentration is of the order of 500 kg/m^3 or even more. Such heavy sediment concentration changes the characteristics of the fluid drastically and modifies the hydraulics of the river. Hence in China hyperconcentration flows have attracted the attention of many research engineers. The First International Workshop on Flows at Hyperconcentration (142) was held in Beijing in 1985 in which twenty-two papers were presented on the following themes :

1. Properties of Flow at Hyperconcentration of Sediment.
2. Velocity Distribution, Resistance and Mechanism of Flow at Hyperconcentration.
3. Transport and Deposition Characteristics of Hyperconcentration Flows.
4. Density Currents — Their Formation, Characteristics and Effect on Reservoir Operations.

It may be mentioned here that a large volume of research work carried out in China on sediment transport and river processes has been reviewed in two excellent books written in Chinese by Ning Chien on these subjects (211, 212). Similarly recently published collection of translation of papers on Lower Yellow River (298) gives valuable information on morphology and regulation of the Lower Yellow River.

LOCAL SCOUR

Local scour attracted the attention of many investigators during this period. As in other cases, the trend was to collect additional data from laboratory studies and the field, and analyse them together. Also some form of analytical or semianalytical approach to scour prediction was adopted. The empirical equations developed for equilibrium scour below the original bed level can be grouped under the following four categories:

Group	Form of Equation	Investigators
I	$D_{se}/D = f(b/D)$	Breusers, Laursen and Toch, Larras, Ettema (78)
II	$D_{se}/D = A_1 (U/\sqrt{gD})^{x1} - (b/D)^{x2}$	Shen, Venkatadri, Shen et al., Jain, Hancu
III	$D_{se}/D = A_2 (U/\sqrt{gD})^{x3} (b/D)^{x4} - 1.0$	Blench, Inglis, Ahmed, Garde, Arunachalam
IV	$D_{se}/D = A_3 (U/\sqrt{gd})^2 - A_4 (d/D)$	Bata, Yaroslavtziev

Here D_{se} is the equilibrium scour depth below the original bed level, D is the depth of flow, U is the mean velocity of flow, b is the pier width or diameter and d is the sediment size.

Major contribution to scour studies during this period are by Qadar (229), Baker (17), Hjorth (127), Ettema (78), Kothyari (100) and S. Hancu. The most popular mechanism suggested for the scour around piers is the formation of horse-shoe vortex. Ettema has experimentally evaluated the effect of sediment non-uniformity and stratification on scour depth. Kothyari (100) has proposed a numerical scheme to calculate scour depth as a function of time, which can be used even when the flow is unsteady due to increase or decrease of discharge. He has also obtained experimentally the correction coefficients to be used in case of non-uniform sediments and stratification of the bed. Based on a large volume of laboratory and field data, he has obtained the following equations for the scour depth.

Scour depth in sediment transporting flows

$$D_{se}/d = 0.99 \left(\frac{b}{d}\right)^{0.67} \left(\frac{D}{d}\right)^{0.40} \alpha^{-0.30}$$

Clear water scour

$$D_{sc}/d = 0.66 \left(\frac{b}{d}\right)^{0.75} \left(\frac{D}{d}\right)^{0.16} \left(\frac{U^2 - U_c^2}{\frac{\Delta\gamma_s}{\rho_s} d}\right)^{0.4} \alpha^{-0.30} \qquad (72)$$

and

$$U_c^2 \Big/ \frac{\Delta\gamma_s}{\rho_f} d = 1.20 \left(\frac{b}{d}\right)^{-0.11} \left(\frac{D}{d}\right)^{0.16}$$

SEDIMENT SAMPLING

Major progress in the area of sediment sampling is the use of nuclear techniques in sediment transport and sedimentation problems. Three nuclear techniques have been tried and found useful. The first deals with the use of nucleonic transmission and backscatter probes for gauging temporal variations in the high suspended sediment concentrations of water courses, and for spatial mapping of soft bed deposits. The second deals with the role of artificial radioisotopes as sediment tracers to reveal the behaviour of silts, sands and gravels. The third is the use of lead-210 dating and artificial fall-out studies in establishing the time scale of recent sedimentations. These techniques along with their shortcomings and advantages are well described in the UNESCO publication by Crickmore *et al.* (50).

Long Yuqian (191) has referred to pressure difference type samplers (similar to Helley Smith Sampler) developed on the Yangtze river. Three samplers named as Changjiang 78-1, 78-2 and 78-3 weigh 15 kg, 50 kg and 100 kg respectively and are used for low, medium and high velocities. Their efficiency is about 60 per cent. Slot or Pit type sampler is described by Emmett (73) where concrete trough or trench 0.4 m by 0.6 m is constructed across the width of about 20 m. The slot is divided into eight sections fitted with gates. Along the bottom of the concrete trough a rubber belt 0.30 m wide is threaded around some drive and guidance pulley which then returns overhead. Sediment falling into the open slot is carried laterally to a sump in the river bank. After continuous sieving and weighing, the sediment is returned to the river downstream of the trap by the conveyor belt. It is used mainly for relatively smaller rivers.

CONTRITBUTIONS BY GEOLOGISTS

During the past half century geologists and geographers have contributed to our understanding of various aspects of alluvial rivers. Geomorphology is the branch of physiography dealing with the lands of earth's surface. This science was formally introduced by Davis but its foundation was laid earlier by Powell, Dutton and Gilbert. One of the most important concepts in geomorphology is that of geomorphic cycle or the cycle of erosion, in which the topography starts with a nearly flat surface which is warped and brought above the sea level by the process of diastrophism. This is followed by erosion due to rain and surface run off, the eroded material is transported through gullies and streams to the sea and in this process the land mass is lowered until, after sufficiently long time, it reduces to a gently sloping plain called peneplain. The whole process is then repeated. This concept has been questioned on some accounts. In this connection the contributions of Penck, King and Hack should be read.

Another concept given by the geomorphologists to the field of Fluvial Hydraulics is that of a graded stream or a stream in equilibrium. J. Hoover Mackin (1905-1968) was the first to give its definition (192). The geomorphologists have also classified streams into young, mature and old streams depending on their characteristics and these have been well described by Lobeck (190). In recent times significant contributions have been made by geologists. Luna Bergere Leopold (1915-) and Thomas Maddock Jr (1907-) have studied the variations of width, depth and velocity along the river length at a specified discharge, e.g., mean annual discharge, and at a section with change in discharge (185). Walter Basil Langbein (1907-) applied (179) the concepts of statistics to determine the exponents in the relations

$$W = aQ^b,\ D = cQ^e,\ U = KQ^m$$

Some what different approach has been used by Knighton (163) to obtain these exponents.

Still another area in which geologists have contributed to Fluvial Hydraulics is in describing river-net in a basin. For this, the concept of stream order has been introduced by R.E. Horton, A.N. Strahler and N.A. Rzhanitsyn. On the basis of this, Horton has proposed three basic laws which deal with how number, average length and average drainage area of streams of given order vary with stream order.

It will be appropriate to mention here the contributions of John Roberts Lawrence Allen and Stanley A. Schumm to Fluvial Hydraulics.

J.R.L. Allen
(1932-)

John Roberts Lawrence Allen was born in 1932 in UK and received his B.Sc. and D.Sc. degrees in geology from the University of Sheffield. He started his academic career in the University of Reading and was elevated to the rank of professor of geology in 1972. He was elected the fellow of the Royal Society in 1979. Since 1988 he is director of the Post Graduate Research Institute for Sedimentology in the University of Reading.

Allen has done extensive research on old sand stone, sedimentary structures, recent sediments with special reference to deltas, and recent sediments and geoarchaelogy of the Severn Estuary. However, his research on sedimentary structures is of direct interest to those working in Fluvia Hydraulics. His studies related to sedimentary structures include character and classification of bed forms, their hierarchies, geometry of current ripples, flute marks, instability of an upper phase plane bed, phase difference between bed forms and flow, and superposition of bed forms. Allen is also the author of books on Current Ripples (1968), Physical Processes of Sedimentation

(1970), Sedimentary Structures (1983), and Principles of Physical Sedimentology (1985).

In his book on Current Ripples, Allen has attempted to describe some of the properties, modes of behaviour, and the role of ripple marks found wherever sand is transported by water. Some of the aspects covered in this book about the current ripples are bed forms and facies analysis, surface anatomy of ripple marks, cross stratification, causes and hydraulic limits of ripple marks, flow past negative steps, and deposition in the ripple lee.

The two-volume work on Sedimentary Structures gives a comprehensive summary and review of what is known about the sedimentary structures; it describes the most important of these structures and offers an explanation for them in terms of general principles. While the first volume deals with the sedimentary structures occurring under relatively simple situations, the second volume deals with sedimentary structures under complex flows such as meanders, jets, and gravity-current surges.

Critical study of Allen's books indicates the variety of aspects of fluvial hydraulics on which he has focussed his attention. These aspects include erosion of cohesive bed, packing of particles of spheroidal and other shapes, orientation and stability of spherical shells settling in water at low Reynolds numbers, the parting lineations on the flat bed and their relation to vortices near the bed, movement and dimensions of the ripples and dunes, geometric and lithological attributes of cross stratification caused by the movement of ripples on dunes, bed forms under changing flow conditions, and flow in river bends with respect to grain size variation across the radius. Of particular interest is the presentation of slightly modified form of $\tau_0 U$ vs d diagram proposed earlier by Simons for predicting regimes of flow. Instead of d, Allen has used effective median physical diameter at 25°C and found the resulting diagram to be slightly superior. His equation for the dimensionless dune height as a function of $\tau_0 / (\gamma_s - \gamma_f)\, d$ also seems to give slightly better accuracy than the other equations.

Stanley A. Schumm is at present professor of geology at the Colorado State University, Fort Çollins (USA). Earlier he worked for the US Geological Survey. He did experimental work on drainage basin evolution, river morphology, hydrology, alluvial-fan, fan-delta, river channel morphology, and sedimentology. These experimental findings have been related to the prototype conditions. In addition, he has also worked on geomorphic thresholds, modification of the erosion cycle, rates of denudation, paleohydrology, effect of sediment type and concentration on channel dimensions and form, and effect of changes in hydrologic regimen on river adjustment. His work is more akin to the contributions of hydraulic engineers and is summarised in the three books on The Fluvial System (1977), River Morphology (1982), and Experimental Fluvial Geomorphology (1987).

Annual geomorphology symposia are helds in the Department of Geological Sciences at the State University of New York at Bringhamton, USA. Their proceedings for the years 1971 and 1973 contain valuable information on quantitative geomorphology and fluvial geomorphology. In addition some books published on River Morphology, Fluvial Processes and Fluvial Systems give good summaries of the contributions of geologists and geographers. Following are some of these books published by geologists, geographers and engineers during this period :

1. Schumm, S.A. The Fluvial System. John Wiley and Sons, New York, 1977.
2. Gregory, K. J. (Ed.). River Channel Changes . John Wiley and Sons, New York, 1977.
3. Shen H. W. (Ed.). Modelling of Rivers. John Wiley and Sons, New York, 1979.
4. Jansen, P.Ph., L. Van Bendegom, J. Van den Berg, M. de Vries, and A. Zanen. Principles of River Engineering: The Non-Tidal Alluvial River. Pitman Publishing Ltd., London, 1979.
5. Rachocki, A. Alluvial Fans: An Attempt at an Empirical Approach. John Wiley and Sons, New York, 1981.
6. Richards, R.K. Rivers: Forms and Processes in Alluvial Channels. Routledge Chapman and Hall, Inc., 1982.
7. Schumm, S.A. River Morphology. Van Nostrand Reinhold, USA, 1982.
8. Allen, J. R. L. Sedimentary Structures : Their Character and Physical Basis. Vol. I and II Elsevier, Amsterdam, 1982
9. Collison, J.D. and J. Lewin. Modern and Ancient Fluvial Systems. Sp. Publ. Int Assoc. of Sedimentologists, 1983.
10. Dingman, S.L. Fluvial Hydrology. Freeman, New York, 1984.
11. Hadley, R.F. and D.E. Walling (Ed.). Erosion and Sediment Yield : Some Methods of Measurement and Modelling. Geo. Books. Norwich, UK, 1984.
12. Knighton, D. Fluvial Forms and Processes. Edward Arnold Ltd. London, UK, 1984.
13. Allen J. R. L. Principles of Physical Sedimentology. George Allen and Unwin Ltd., London. 1985.
14. Schumm, S.A., M.P. Mosley and W.E. Weaver. Experimental Fluvial Morphology. A Wiley Interscience Publication. John Wiley and Sons, New York. 1987.
15. Chang, H.H. Fluvial Processes in River Engineering. John Wiley and Sons. New York, 1988.
16. Russel, R.J. River and Delta Morphology. Louisiana State University Studies, USA.

17. Mangelsdorf, J., K. Scheurmann and F.H. Weiss. River Morphology: A Guide for Geoscientists and Engineers. Springer Verlag, Berlin, 1990.

MISCELLANEOUS

It will be useful to comment briefly on some aspects which have helped the growth of Fluvial Hydraulics and the dissemination of information.

The first is the holding of bilateral seminars and workshops between two countries in order to exchange experience and discuss common problems. Such a bilateral seminar between Japan and China was held in Japan in August 1984, in which River Hydraulics and Engineering Experiences were discussed. Similar workshop between UK and India on Sediment Measurement and Control was held in February 1988 at Chandigarh (India).

The other aspect is the starting of the International Journal of Sediment Research by International Research and Training Centre for Erosion and Sedimentation (IRTCES) in 1986. The themes covered in the Journal include not only mechanics of sediment transportation and fluvial processes, but also include matters related to geography, geomorphology, soil erosion, sediment yield, soil conservation, environmental and ecological impact of sedimentation, and social and economic impacts of sedimentation. This journal has provided an excellent opportunity to share experience in erosion and sedimentation with fellow engineers.

The third aspect relates to the holding of International Symposia on River Sedimentation by IRTCES every three years. The first symposim was held in Beijing in 1980 and the subsequent symposia were held in 1983, 1986, 1989 and 1992 in China, U.S.A., China and Germany respectively. The themes chosen for these symposia give some indication about priority areas of research in Fluvial Hydraulics. Some of these themes are Sediment Yield and Utilisation, Fluvial Processes (including estuarine and coastal sedimentation), Reservoir Sedimentation, Laboratory and Field Measuring Techniques, Hydraulics of Alluvial Rivers , Sediment Transportation in Rivers, River Training, Model Investigations and Prototype Measuring Techniques, River and Coastal Hydrodynamics, Methodologies in Sediment Research, Mathematical Modelling, Small Watershed Management and its Benefits, Environmental Impact of Erosion and Sedimentation, and Socio-Economic and Institutional Aspects of Sedimentation.

With a large number of engineers and scientists working on various aspects of Fluvial Hydraulics, it is very difficult to do full justice in mentioning the contribution made by the individuals; this is also true because it is only after some period that the importance of the findings and their implication on the development of Fluvial Hydraulics can be assessed. However, it will still be more appropriate to mention the names of some of them such as W.R. White, P. Ackers, I. Beechi, W. Bechteler, S. Bruk, V. Subramanian, R.I. Ferguson, S. Komura, M.G. Wolman, C.T. Yang, M. Vetter, Fan Jiahua, J. Zeller, W. Schrimpf, G. Holtroff, S.N. Ghosh,

S. Hancu, B.M. Sumer, M. Bayazit, P.A. Mantz, J.C. Willis, W.W. Emmett, I. Laczay, H.J. Volmer, C.F. Nordin, J.P. Chollet, R. Bettes, C.C. Song, N.G. Bhowmik,. He Mingmin, Han Qiwei, W. Rodi, N.L. Colemann,G. DiSilvo, A. Lamberti, Long Yuqian, Du Guohan, Zan Qishun, Li Baoru, and others who have enriched the literature on Fluvial Hydraulics through their researches and contributed to our understanding of the complex processes.

The lecture notes on "Introduction to River Engineering" by Jose′ Antonio Maza Alvarez give some indication of the research work done in Mexico by J.A. Maza Alvarez, C. Cruickshank, Flores M.Garcia and others.

An expicit relationship has been suggested between dimensionless critical shear stress and $\frac{u_{*c}d}{\nu}$ and also between the former and $\Delta\gamma_s d^3 / \rho_f \nu^2$. The critical mean velocity has been made dimensionless as $U_c / \sqrt{gd}$ and is expressed as a function of $\Delta\gamma_s / \gamma_f$ and d/R in the power type relationship.

Maza and Cruickshank have proposed resistance relationships for the upper and lower regimes in the form $U / \omega_0 = f\left(\frac{D}{d_{8.4}}, \frac{S}{\Delta\gamma_s / \gamma_f}\right)$ where the regime of flow is predicted by $\frac{1}{S} = f\left(\frac{D\gamma_f}{\Delta\gamma_s\, d_{84}}\right)$. They have also given a diagram between $\frac{US}{\omega_0}$ and DS/d_{84} with D/d_{84} and the regime of flow as the third variables. One interesting relationship given by Maza is about the maximum critical shear stress, a log-normal sediment mixture can withstand in the armoured state. It is given by

$$\tau_{oc} / \Delta\gamma_s\, d_{50} = \left[0.0292\, \sigma_s^{1.62} + 0.042\, e^{-0.65\,\sigma_s}\right] \quad (73)$$

Using different equations for resistance, sediment transport and the bank resistance (relation between B and D), they have proposed equations for the determination of channel dimensions and slope. Lastly, some work has been done on estimation of scour depth at bridge piers, spurs and other structures and on scour protection.

A recent publication (150) of Japan Society of Civil Engineers summarises the salient contributions made by the Japanese hydraulicians in Fluvial Hydraulics during 1980-1990. This report contains chapters on Mud and Debris Flow (by K. Miyamoto and S. Egashira), Hydraulics of Mountain Rivers (by S. Egashira), Sediment Yield (by K. Sawai), Grain Sorting of Sediment (by K. Suzuki), River Bed Configurations (by M. Kuroki), Studies on Channel Changes in Rivers (by K. Hasegawa), Flow in Compound Channels (by A. Tominga and I. Nezu), Observations of Flood Flow and River Bed Evolution (by Y. Shimuzu, Y. Watanabe and S. Yamashita), and Numerical Simulation of Flow and Bed Deformation of River (by T. Itakura and Y. Shimuzu).

A close study of the report indicates that some of the institutes in Japan that are engaged in sediment research are Disaster Prevention Research Institute, Kyoto, Sabo Technical Center at Tokyo, Hydraulics Laboratory of the Hokkaido

University, and Civil Erngineering Research Institute of Hokkaido Development Bureau, both at Sapporo, Nagoya Institute of Technical University, and Public Works Research Institute. Further, the problems that are being investigated are closely related to the problems Japan is facing. Lastly, it indicates that deveopment and use of two- and three- dimensional models for flow around bends, spurs, etc. is actively being done there.

Lastly, strong centres of Research have been developed at some universities and institutes where concerted efforts are being made to further the knowledge in Fluvial Hydraulics. Some such centres are the Delft Hydraulics Laboratory and the Delft University of Technology where M. de Vries, J.S. Ribberink, J.T.M. Van Der Zande, L.C. Van Rijn, C.B. Vreugdenhil, G.S. Klassen and others are working, the Iowa Institute of Hydraulic Research where A.J. Odgaard, S.C. Jain, F.M. Holly Jr., R. Ettema and others are active, Colorado State University, University of Berkeley, S.A.F. Laboratory, Hydraulic Research Institute of Wallingford (UK), the University of Caterburry at Christchurch (N.Z.) where A J. Sutherland and others are working, and Institute of Hydrodynamics and Hydraulic Engineering, Technnical University of Denmark. Similar institutes exist in China, Russia, France, Germany, and other countries. Such planned efforts by a large number of institutes have accelerated the pace of research and have also helped in better understanding of various aspects of Fluvial Hydraulics and in seeking solution to complex problems.

CONCLUDING REMARKS

All round progress in the development of Fluvial Hydraulics was made during this period. Soil erosion, scour, planform analysis, mathematical modelling in straight as well as curved reaches of rivers, reservoir sedimentation, armouring, and flows with hyper-concentration were paid due attention. A large number of researchers and institutes participated in this endeavour and there was a higher level of international cooperation among the investigators. Several centres of excellence developed all over the world in the universities as well as in government research institutes. Considerable effort must have gone in research in former USSR and East European countries but full justice could'nt be done here because of language barrier and other difficulties.

Chapter 9

Epilogue

Even though people in general were aware of the sediment problems in earlier times and were handling the same to the best of their ability, one can for all practical purpose accept that the science of Fluvial Hydraulics started in 1879 with the development of bed-load equation by du Boys. In less than 125 years significant progress has been made in understanding the complex phenomena, developing the mathematical frame work and finding working solutions.

One can now prepare a stage discharge curve for a natural stream for given slope, size distribution of the bed material and channel characteristics. Similarly one can now prepare stage vs bed-load or total load curve for a stream for each size of bed material. Flow in a bend has been analysed and it is now possible to determine the lateral bed profile at any section along the bend. It is also possible to determine the progressive scour around a bridge pier under unsteady flow condition and also the maximum scour that can take place. Having known the equations of motion, method of small disturbances has been used to study formation of ripples, dunes and antidunes, alternate bars and sediment sorting. Attempts have been made to develop computer codes for studying transients in alluvial streams with single as well multiple connected channels, and migration of meanders. Some progress has also been made to study sedimentation in settling tanks using turbulence models. Stochastic methods are increasingly used in the study of various phenomena in Fluvial Hydraulics. Also, optimisation techniques have been used to explain channel adjustments and formation of meandering and braiding.

Some land-marks (157) in the development of Fluvial Hydraulics can be listed. These are :

1. du Boy's bed-load equation
2. Gilbert's experimental work
3. Exner's analysis of bed deformation
4. Shields' analysis of critical tractive force
5. Lacey's regime analysis

6. Development of suspended sediment concentration distribution equation
7. Meyer-Peter, Müller's bed-load equation
8. Einstein and Barbarossa's resistance analysis
9. Einstein's bed-load function
10. Regime criteria for macro-scale and mesos scale bed forms
11. Stability analysis applied to bed undulations and plan forms
12. Development of computer codes e.g. HEC-6 and CHARIMA

The question that comes to the mind at this stage is: In which direction will the developments take place in Fluvial Hydraulics in future? Past experience in other branches of science and engineering indicates that it is quite difficult and even dangerous to predict the way in which developments would take place in a particular branch in the next two to four decades. Who would have correctly predicted the developments in nuclear physics, bio-technology, space technology and computers say 50 years back? However, one can venture to make a few short term predictions and modify them with the passage of time.

It seems that the research in Fluvial Hydraulics at micro level has nearly reached the stage of diminishing returns and hence one can anticipate lesser efforts in that direction unless detailed measurements of turbulence in water and sediment phases are done. The same can be said about resistance and sediment transport under steady uniform flow conditions. However, since the present day methods in predicting resistance and transport give errors of the order of ± 30 per cent or so, there is a need to increase the accuracy of prediction. Here one would be tempted to use the brute force of computers to develop regression equations which may completely disregard the physics of the problem and obtain equation or equations which may be more accurate predictors. Some other areas in which research may progress:

- Indirect and cheaper bank protection methods which would depend on development of appropriate circulation near banks;
- Applicability of instability theory to other aspects of Fluvial Hydraulics;
- Combination of hydrologic, hydraulic modelling and erosion to predict Q and Q_T hydrographs for the river;
- Transient flow in braided channels where braided pattern is changing;
- Studies similar to the above but for a basin involving more number of streams;
- Sediment transport under unsteady non-uniform flow condition;
- Effect of cohesivity on the channel geometry;
- More rational design methods for sediment excluders and ejectors;

- Use of stochastic modelling and optimisation in other aspects of fluvial Hydraulics;
- Modelling of meandering by inclusion of spatial distribution of lithology;
- Newer techniques of bed-load and total load measurement;
- Greater use of remote sensing in study of river behaviour;
- Development of better and newer techniques of sediment removal from reservoirs and disposal of sediment;
- Fluid sediment interaction — how presence of sediment affects the turbulence characteristics and vice-versa;
- Rationalisation of different methods of designing movable bed models; and
- Environmental impact analysis of fluvial processes, erosion control over larger areas.

References

1. Abbott, M.B. and J.A. Cunge (Eds). Engineering Applications of Computational Hydraulics: Vol. 1. Homage to Alexandre Preissmann. Pitman Advanced Publishing Programme, Pitman Publishing Inc. 1982.
2. Ackers, P. and W.R. White. Sediment Transport: New Approach and Analysis. JHD, Proc. ASCE, Vol. 99, No. Hy-11, Nov. 1973.
3. Alam, Z.U., and J.F. Kennedy. Friction Factors for Flow in Sand-Bed Channels. JHD, Proc. ASCE, Vol. 95, No. Hy-6, Nov. 1969
4. Albertson, M.L., D.B. Simons, and E.V. Richardson. Discussion of Paper by H.K.Liu on 'Mechanics of Ripple Formation'. JHD, Proc. ASCE, Vol. 84, No. Hy-l, Feb. 1958.
5. Allen, J.R.L. Current Ripples: Their Relation to Patterns of Water and Sediment Motion. North-Holl and Publishing Company, Amsterdam, 1968.
6. Allen, J.R.L. Sedimentary Structures: Their Character and Physical Basis. Elsevier Science Publishers, The Netherlands, Vol. 1, 1984.
7. Anderson, A. G. Distribution of Suspended Sediment in a Natural Stream. Trans. AGU, Vol. 23, Pt. II, 1942.
8. Antsyferov, S.M. and R. D. Kosyan. Sediment Suspended in Stream Flow. JHD, Proc. ASCE, Vol. 106, No. HY-2, Feb. 1980.
9. Apmann, R.P and R.M. Rumer. Diffusion of Sediment in Developing Flow. JHD, Proc. ASCE, Vol. 96, No. Hy-1, Jan. 1970
10. Argyropoulos, P.A. On the Most Important Ancient Greek Contribution to the History of Hydraulics: The Fundamental Law of Flow $Q = AU$. Proc. of 17th Congress of IAHR, Baden-Baden, S-54, Vol. 6, 1977.
11. Asawa, G.L., K.G. Ranga Raju and R.J. Garde. Sediment Transport in Aggrading Streams. Proc. 2nd Int. Workshop on Alluvial River Problems. University of Roorkee, India, 1985.
12. Asawa, G.L. and K.G. Ranga Raju. Some Aspects of Sediment Transport in Non-equilibrium Flows. Proc. 3rd Int. Workshop on Alluvial River Problems. University of Roorkee, India, 1989.
13. Ashida, K. and M. Michiue. An Investigation of River Degradation Downstream of a Dam. Proc. of 14th Congress of IAHR, Paris, Vol. 3, 1971.
14. Ashida, K. and M. Michiue. Studies on Bed-Load Transport Rate in Open Channel Flows. Proc. of Int. Symposium on River Mechanics, IAHR, Bangkok, Vol. 1, 1973.
15. Bagnold, R.A. Flow of Cohesionless Grains in Fluids Philosophical Trans. R S L, No. 964, Vol. 249, 1956.
16. Bagnold, R.A. An Approach to the Sediment Transport from General Physics. USGS Professional Paper 422-1, 1966.
17. Baker, C.J. Theoretical Prediction of Local Scour Around Bridge Piers. JHR, IAHR, Vol. 18, No. 1, 1980.
18. Baumgarten, M. Navigation Fluviale Garonne. Annales des Ponts et Chausse'es , 2, 1848.

19. Bayazit, M. Simulation of Armour Coat Formation and Destruction. Proc. of 16th Congress of IAHR, Sao Paulo, (Brazil), Vol. 2, 1975.
20. Bell, J.R. The Continuous Bund and Apron Method of Protecting the Flanks of Bridges for Rivers in the Punjab. 25th Aug. 1890.
21. Bell, R.G. and A.J. Sutherland. Non-equilibrium Bed-Load Transport by Steady Flow. JHE, Proc. ASCE, Vol. 109, No. 3, Mar. 1983.
22. Belleudy, P. Last Ten Years' LHF Experience in Developing River Sediment Simulation Software. Proc. Int. Symp. on East-West, North-South State of the Art in River Engineering Methods and Design Philosophies. Vol. 1, St. Petersburg, Russia, May, 1994.
23. Bendict, P.C., M.L. Albertson and D.Q. Matejka. Total Sediment Load Measured in Turbulence Flume. Trans. ASCE, Vol. 120, 1955.
24. Bharat Singh, Bed-Load Transport in Channels. JIP, CBIP (India), Vol. 18, No. 5, May 1961.
25. Bharat Singh. Bed-Load Transport in Channels. JIP, CBIP (India), Vol. 21, No. 5, May 1964
26. Blasius, H. Uber die Abhangigkeit der Formen der Riffeln und Geschiebebanke Von Gefalle. Z. Bauwesen, Jgg. LX, 1910.
27. Blench, T. and C. King. Effect of Dynamic Shape on Lacey Relation. Annual Report (T), Central Board of Irrigation, New Delhi (India), 1941.
28. Bondurant, D.C. Sedimentation Studies of the Conchas Reservoir in New Mexico. Proc. ASCE, (Separate) No. 29, 1950.
29. Borland, W.M. and C.R. Miller. Distribution of Sediment in Large Reservoirs. JHD, Proc. ASCE, Vol. 84, No. HY-2, Apr. 1958.
30. Brebner, A. and K.C. Wilson. Derivation of Regime Equation from Relationships for Pressurised Flow by Use of the Principle of Minimum Energy Degradation Rate. Proc. ICE (London), Vol. 36, 1967.
31. Brooks, N.H. Mechanics of Streams with Movable Beds of Fine Sands. Trans. ASCE, Vol. 123, 1958.
32. Brooks, N.H. Calculation of Suspended Load Discharge From Velocity and Concentration Parameters. Proc. FIASC, USDA, Washington, Paper No. 29, 1963.
33. Brown, C.B. The Control of Reservoir Silting, USDA, Miscellaneous publication 521, 1943.
34. Brune, G. M. Trap Efficiency of Reservoirs. Trans. AGU, Vol. 34, No. 3, July 1953.
35. Bruk, S. (Ed.) Methods of Computing Sedimentation in Lakes and Reservoirs. A Contribution to IHP-II Project A.2.6.1 Panel, UNESCO, Feb. 1985.
36. Buckley, A.B. The Influence of Silt on the Velocity of Water in Open Channels. Proc. ICE (London), Vol. 216, 1922.
37. Callander, R.A. Instability and River Channels, JFM, Vol. 36, Pt.3, 1969.
38. Central Board of Irrigation and Power. Manual of River Behaviour, Control and Training. Pub. No. 60, New Delhi (India), 1956.
39. Central Board of Irrigation and Power. Efficiency of Suspended Load Samplers. Tech. Rep. No. 13, New Delhi (India), 1974.
40. Celik, I. and W. Rodi. Simulation of Hydrodynamic and Transport Characteristics of Rectangular Settling Basins. Proc. of Euromech 192, Transport of Suspended Solids in Open Channels. Munich (Neubiberg), June 1985.
41. Chang, H.H. Stable Alluvial Channel Design. JHD, Proc. ASCE, Vol. 106, No. Hy-5, May, 1980.
42. Chang, Y.L. Laboratory Investigation of Flume Traction and Transportation, Trans. ASCE, Vol. 104, 1939.
43. Chevray, R. Robert G. Kennedy and the Regime Theory. Proc. of 17th Congress of IAHR, Baden-Baden, Vol. 6, S-5, 14, 1977.
44. Chitale, S. V. Design of Alluvial Channels; Proc. of 6th Congress of ICID, Q. 20, R. 17, N. Delhi, 1966.
45. Chitale, S. V. Hydraulics of Stable Channels. CBIP, New Delhi, 1966.
46. Clavel, M. Notice Sur M. Fargue. Annales des Ponts et Chausseés, No. 75, 1910.

47. Colby, B.R. and C.H. Hembree. Computations of Total Sediment Discharge, Niobrara River, near Cody, Nebraska. USGS Water Supply Paper 135, 1955.
48. Colby, B.R. and R.P. Chirstensen. Visual Accumulation Tube for Size Analysis of Sands. JHD, Proc. ASCE, No. HY-3, June, 1956.
49. Coleman, N.C. Velocity Profiles with Suspended Sediments. JHR, IAHR, Vol. 19, No. 3, 1981.
50. Crickmore, M.J., G.S. Tazioli, P.G. Appleby and F. Oldfield. The Use of Nuclear Techniques in Sediment Transport and Sedimentation Problems. Technical Documents in Hydrology, IHP Programme, UNESCO, Paris, 1990.
51. Cunningham, A. Roorkee Hydraulics Experiments. Proc. ICE (London), Vol. 71, 1882.
52. Daily, J.W. Obituary of A. T. Ippen. JHR, IAHR, Vol. 12, No. 2, 1974.
53. Davies, B.E. Armouring of Alluvial Beds. M E Thesis, University of Canterbury, Christchurch, N.Z., 1974.
54. de Vries, M. Application of Physical and Mathematical Models for River Problems. Publ. No. 112, Delft Hyd. Laboratory, Delft, 1973.
55. Ding Lianzhen and Zhou Zhide. Lecture Notes on Mathematical Modelling for Reservoir Sedimentation. IRTCES Course on Reservoir Sedimentation, N. Delhi, 1991.
56. Dobbins, W.E. Effect of Turbulence on Sedimentation. Trans. ASCE, Vol. 109, 1941 (See also discussion by McNown, J S).
57. duBoys, P.F.D. Le Rhone et les Rivieres a Lit Affouillable. Annales des Ponts et Chausseés (5) 18, 1879.
58. Dunn, I.S. Tractive Resistance of Cohesive Channels. JSM, Proc. ASCE, SM-3, June, 1959.
59. Dupuit, H.P. Traite de la Conduite et de la Distribution de Eau. Paris, 1865.
60. Einstein, H.A., A.G. Anderson, and J. W. Johnson. Distinction Between Bed-Load and Suspended Load in Natural Streams. Trans. AGU, Vo. 21, 1940.
61. Einstein, H.A. Formula for the Transportation of Bed-Load. Trans. ASCE, Vol. 107, 1942.
62. Einstein, H.A. Conformity between Model and Prototype: A Symposium Discussion. Trans. ASCE, Vol. 109, 1944.
63. Einstein, H.A and R.B. Banks. Fluid Resistance of Composite Roughness. Trans. AGU, Vol. 31, No. 4, Aug. 1950.
64. Einstein, H.A. The Bed-Load Function for Sediment Transportation in Open Channel Flows. USDA, Tech. Bull. No. 1026, Sept. 1950.
65. Einstein, H.A. and N.L. Barbarossa. River Channel Roughness. Trans. ASCE, Vol. 117, 1952.
66. Einstein, H.A. and Ning Chien. Transport of Sediment Mixtures with Large Range of Grain Sizes. IER, MRD Series No. 2, 1953.
67. Einstein, H.A. and Ning Chien. Second Approximation to the Solution of the Suspended Load Theory. IER, MRD Series No. 2, 1954.
68. Einstein, H.A. and Ning Chien. Effect of Heavy Sediment Concentration Near Bed on the Velocity and Sediment Distribution. IER, MRD series No. 8, 1955.
69. Einstein, H.A. and Ning Chien. Similarity of Distorted River Models with Movable Beds. Trans. ASCE, Vol. 121, 1956.
70. Einstein. E.R. (Mrs). Discussion of Ref. 249, JHD, Proc. ASCE, Vol. 102, No. Hy-l, Jan. 1976.
71. Egiazaroff, I.V. Calculation of Non-uniform Sediment Concentration. JHD, Proc. ASCE, Vol. 91, No. Hy-4, July, 1965.
72. Elwell, H.A. A Soil Loss Estimation Technique for South Africa. In "Soil Conservation: Problems and Prospects. John Wiley and Sons. Chichester, U.K., 1981.
73. Emmett, W.W. Field Calibration of the Sediment Trapping Characteristics of Helley Smith Bed-Load Sampler. USGS. Open File Rep. 79-411, 1979.
74. Engelund, F. Hydraulic Resistance of Alluvial Streams. JDH, Proc. ASCE, Vol. 92, No. Hy-2, Mar. 1966.
75. Engelund, F. and E. Hansen. A Monograph on Sediment Transport in Alluvial Streams. Teknisk Forlag, Denmarks, 1967.

76. Engelund, F. Flow and Bed Topography in Channel Bends. JHD, Proc. ASCE, Vol. 100, No. Hy-II, Nov. 1974.

77. Engelund, F. and O. Skovgaard. On the Origin of Meandering and Braiding in Alluvial Streams. JFM, Vol. 97, Pt. 2, 1973.

78. Ettema, R. Scour at Bridge Sites. Report No. 117, University of Auckland, N.Z. 1980.

79. Everest, R. Some Observations on the Quantity of Earth Matter Brought Down by the Ganges River. Asiatic Society of Bengal, Jour. No. 1, 1832.

80. Exner, F.M. Uber die Wechselwirkung Zwischen Wasser und Geschiebe in Flussen. Sitzungsberiahte de Akademie der Wissenschaften in Wien. Pt IIa, 134, 1925.

81. Fan, C.H. A Study of Stable Channel Cross Sections. Hydraulic Engineering, Chinese Society of Civil Engineers, Vol. 15, 1947.

82. Forchheimer, Ph. Experiments on Accumulation of Transported Sedimentary Material in the Convex River Bends. Hyd. Lab. Practice, ASME, 1928.

83. Foster, G.R., W.H. Neibling and R.A. Nattermann. A Programmable Rainfall Simulator. Paper No. 82-2570, ASAE, St. Joseph, Michigan, 1982.

84. Franke, P.G. and A. Kleinschroth (Eds.) Kurzbiographien Hydraulik und Wasserbau, Personlichkeiten Aus Dem Deutschsprachichen Raun Karl M. Lipp. Verlag, Munchen 1991.

85. Freèman, J.R.(Ed.), Hydraulic Laboratory Practice. ASME, New York, 1928.

86. Friedkin, J.F. A Laboratory Study of Meandering of Alluvial Rivers. USWES. Vicksburg,. Miss. (USA) 1945.

87. Gales, R. The Principles of River Training for Railway Bridges and Their Application to the Case of Hardinge Bridge Over the Lower Ganges at Sara. Jour. Institution of Civil Engineers (London), Paper No. 5167, Dec. 1938.

88. Garde, R.J. and M. L. Albertson. Discussion of Laursen's Paper. Ref. 180, JHD, Proc. ASCE; Vol. 84, No. Hy-6, Nov. 1958.

89. Garde, R.J. and M.L. Albertson. Sand Waves and Regimes of Flow in Alluvial Channels. Proc. of 8th Congress of IAHR, Montreal (Canada), Vol. 4, 1959.

90. Garde, R.J. Total Sediment Transport in Alluvial Channels. Ph.D. Thesis, Colorado State University, Fort Collins (USA), 1959.

91. Garde, R.J. and M.L. Albertson. Bed-Load Transport in Alluvial Channels. La Houille Blanche, No. 3, 1961.

92. Garde, R.J. and J. Dattatri. Investigations of the Total Sediment Discharge of Alluvial Streams. University of Roorkee Research Journal, Roorkee, Vol. 6, No. 2, 1963.

93. Garde, R.J. and K.G. Ranga Raju. Resistance Relationships for Alluvial Channel Flow. JHD, Proc. ASCE, Vol. 92, No. Hy-4, July 1966.

94. Garde, R. J. and S.M. Hasan. An Experimental Investigation of Degradation in Alluvial Channels. Proc. of 12th Congress of IAHR, Fort Collins, (U.S.A.), Vol. 3, 1967.

95. Grade R.J., K. A. Shaikh Ali and S. Diette. Armouring Process in Degrading Streams. JHD, Proc. ASCE, Vol. 103, No. Hy-9, Sept.1977.

96. Grade, R. J. Irrigation in Ancient Meospotamia. Bulletin of Int. Commission on Irrigation and Drainage, No. 2, July 1978.

97. Grade, R. J., K.G. Ranga Raju., P. K. Swamee., G.D. Miraki, and M. Molanezhad. Mathematical Modelling of Sedimentation Process in Reservoir and Upstream Reaches. Hyd. Engg. Rep. No. HYD 8304, University of Roorkee, 1983.

98. Garde, R. J. and U. C. Kothyari. Erosion in Indian Catchments. 3rd Int.Symposium on River Sedimentation — Jackson (Miss), USA, 1986.

99. Garde, R.J. and Anil Kumar. Verification of Regime Criteria for Alluvial Streams. Indo-British Workshop on Sediment Measurement and Control. Chandigarh (Punjab), Feb. 1988.

100. Garde, R. J., K. G. Ranga Raju and U. C Kothyari. Research Report on Effect of Unsteadiness and Stratification on Local Scour. Civil Engg. Dept., University of Roorkee, Roorkee, March 1989.

101. Garde, R. J. and K. G. Ranga Raju. Mechanics of Sediment Transportation and Alluvial Stream Problems. Wiley Eastern Ltd. Publishers, 2nd Edition, N. Delhi, 1985.

102. Garde, V. G. Contribution of Ancient India to the Art and Science of River Mechanics and Management. Jour. of the Inst. of Engineers (India), Vol. 55, Cl, 5-6, May, 1975.

103. Garrett, A. Hydraulic Diagrams for Design of Channels in Earth by Kutter's Formula, 2nd Ed. 1913.

104. Gessler, J. The Beginning of Bed-Load Movement of Mixtures Investigated as Natural Armouring in Channels. Rep. No. 69, Laboratory and Hydraulic Research and Soil Mechanics, Swiss Federal Institute of Technology, Dec. 1965.

105. Gessler, J. Self Stabilising Tendencies of Alluvial Channels. JWHD, Proc. ASCE, Vol. 96, No. WW-2, May, 1970.

106. Gilbert, G. K. The Sufficiency of Terrestrial Rotation for the Deflection of Streams. Nat. Acad. Sc., Vol. 3, Memo. 1, 1884.

107. Gilbert, G. K. The Transportation of Debris by Running Water. Prof. Paper 86, USGS, 1914.

108. Glover, R. E. and Q. L. Florey. Stable Channel Profiles. USBR, Hyd. Lab. Rep. No. 325, 1951.

109. Gottlieb, L. Three Dimensional Flow Pattern and Bed Topography in Meandering Channels. Institute of Hydrodynamics and Hyd. Engg., Technical University of Denmark, Series Paper 1179, 1976.

110. Graf, W. H. and E. R. Acaroglu. Sediment Transport in Conveyance System. JASH Bulletin, Vol. 13, No. 2, 1968.

111. Graf, W. H. Hydraulics of Sediment Transport. McGraw Hill Book Co., New York (USA), 1971, Chapt. 1.

112. Gras, S. Etudes Sur le Torrents des Alps. Anneles des Ponts et Chausseés. No. 2, 1857.

113. Griggs, R. F. The Buffalo River : An Interesting Meandering Stream. Bull. Geo. So. of Am., Vol. 38, No. 3, 1906.

114. Gupta, R. D. Total Sediment Load as a Parameter in the Design of Stable Channels. M E Thesis, Civil Engg. Dept., University of Roorkee, 1967.

115. Hao, Chunyi (Ed.) The Yellow River. China Water Resources and Electric Power Press, Beijing (China), 1987.

116. Hansen, E. On the Formation of the Meanders as a Stability Problem. Coastal Engg. Hydraulics Laboratory, Technical University of Denmark, Rep. No. 13, 1967.

117. Haque, M. I. and K. Mahmood. Analytical Determination of Form Friction Factor, JHE, Proc. ASCE, Vol. 109, No. 4, Apr. 1983.

118. Harrison, A. S. and A. C. Lidicker. Computing Suspended Sand Loads From Field Measurements. FIASC, USDA, Washington, Paper No. 56, 1963.

119. Harza Engg. Co. and Binnie and Partners. Hydrological Survey of Iraq. Vol. 2 of the Final Report, Baghdad, July 1963.

120. Hathaway, G.A. Observations on Channel Changes, Degradation and Scour Below Dams. Proc. of 2nd Congress of IAHR, Stockholm, 1948.

121. Hayami, S. Hydrological Studies on Yangtze River, China II : The Theory of Silt Transportation by Running Water. Jour. of Shanghai Science Institute, Sect. 1, Vol. 1, 1938.

122. Hayashi, T. Study on the Cause of Meandering Rivers. Proc. IAHR Symposium on River Mechanics, Bangkok, Vol. 1, 1973.

123. Hayashi, T. and S. Ozaki. Alluvial Bed Form Analysis I – Formation of Alternate Bars and Braids. Proc. US-Japan Binational Seminar on Erosion and Sedimentation, Hawai, W R Publication, Mar. 1978.

124. Hayashi, T., S. Ozaki and T. Ichibashi. Study on Bed-Load Transportation on Sediment Mixtures. Proc. of 24th Conference of Hydraulics (Japan), 1980.

125. Helley, H. J. and W. Smith. Development and Calibration of the Helley Smith Bed-Load Sampler. USDI, GS Open File Report 79-411, 1979.

126. Hey, R. D., J. C. Bathrust and C. R. Thorne. Gravel Bed Rivers. John Wiley and Sons, New York, 1982.

127. Hjorth, P. Studies on the Nature of Local Scour. Bulletin Series A, No. 46, Dept. of W.R. Engg. Lund Institute of Technology, Lund, Sweden, 1975.

128. Hjlustrom, F. The Morphological Activity of Rivers as Illustrated by River Fyris. Bull. Geo. Inst. Uppsala, Vol. 25, (Chapt. 3), 1935.
129. Hooker, E. H. The Suspension of Solids in Flowing Water. Trans. ASCE, Vol. 36 1896
130. Horton, R. E. Some Better Kutter's Formula Coefficients. Engineering News, Feb. 24, and May 4, 1916.
131. Hoyt, W. G. and W. B. Langbein. Floods. Princeton University Press, Princeton, N J (USA), Chapt. 6, 1955
132. Hubbell, D.W. Apparatus and Techniques of Measuring Bed-Load. USGS, W S Paper 1748, 1964.
133. Hubbell, D. W. and W.W. Sayre. Sand Transport with Radioactive Tracers. JHD,Proc. ASCE, Vol. 90, No. Hy-3, Mar. 1964.
134. Hunt, J. N. The Turbulent Transport of Suspended Sediment in Open Channels. Proc. RSL, Series A, Vol. 224, No. 1158, 1954.
135. Hurst, H.E. The Suspension of Sand in Water. Proc. RSL, Series A, Vol. 157, 1929.
136. IAHR. Proc.of 8th Congress of IAHR, Montreal (Canada), Vol. 4, 1959.
137. IIHR. A Study of Methods Used in Measurement and Analysis of Sediment Loads in Streams. Rept. No 1—Field Practice and Equipment Used in Sampling Suspended Sediment. Univ. of Iowa, USA, 1940.
138. Ilo, G.C. Analytical and Experimental Investigation of River Bed Degradation. Ph.D. Thesis, IIT, Bombay, 1976.
139. Inglis, C. C. The Behaviour and Control of Rivers (with the aid of Models), CWPNRS, Pub. No. 13, Pune (India), 1949.
140. Ippen, A.T. and P. A. Drinker. Boundary Shear Stresses in Curved Trapezoidal Channels. JHD, Proc. ASCE, Vol. 88, No. Hy-5, Sept. 1962.
141. Ippen, A.T. A New Look at Sedimentation in Turbulent Streams. Jour. of the Boston Society of Civil Engineers, U.S.A. Vol. 58, No. 3, July 1971.
142. IRTCES. Proceedings of International Workshop on Flow at Hyperconcentrations of Sediment. Beijing (China), 1985.
143. Itakura, T. and T. Kishi. Open Channel Flow with Suspended Sediments. JHD, Proc.ASCE, Vol. 106, No. HY-8. Aug. 1980.
144. Iwagaki, Y. On the Analysis of Mechanism of River Bed Variation by Characteristics. Memoirs of the Faculty of Engineering. Kyoto University (Japan), Vol. 18, No. 3, July 1956.
145. Iwagaki, Y. Hydrodynamical Study on Critical Tractive Force. Trans JSCE, No. 41, 1956 (In Japanese).
146. Jacobson , T. and R. M. Adams. Salt and Silt in Ancient Mesopotamian Agriculture. Science. Vol. 128, No. 3334, 21st Nov.1958.
147. Jain, S.C. and J. F. Kennedy. Spectral Evolution of Sedimentary Bed Forms. JFM, Vol. 63, 1974.
148. Jaramillo, W. F. and S. C. Jain. Aggradation and Degradation of Alluvial Channel Beds. JHD, Proc. ASCE, Vol. 110, No. Hy-8, 1984.
149. Joshi, G. G. Bharatiya Jalashastra. Shilpa-Sansar, Feb.19, 1955 (In Hindi).
150. JSCE. Research and Practice of Hydraulic Engineering in Japan. No. 5I-2, Fluvial Hydraulics. Jour. of Hydroscience and Hydraulic Engineering, Special Issues/ 1993.
151. Kalinske, A. A. Suspended Material Transport under Nonqulibrium Conditions. Trans.AGU, Pt. II, 1940.
152. Kalinske, A.A. Criteria for Determining Sand Transport by Surface Creep and Saltation. Trans. AGU, 1942.
153. Kalinske, A.A. Movement of Bed-Load in Rivers, Trans. AGU, Vol. 28, No. 4, 1947.
154. Karim, M. F. and F. M. Holly, Jr. Armouring and Sorting Simulation in Alluvial Rivers., JHD, Proc. ASCE Vol. 112, No. 9, 1986.
155. Karman, Th. V. Sand Ripples in the Desert. Technical Book, 1947.
156. Kennedy, J.F. and E.O. Macagno (Ed).Hydraulics, Mechanics of Fluids, Engineering Education — Selected Writings of Hunter Rouse. Dover Publications Inc. New York (USA), 1971.

157. Kennedy, J.F. Whence and Whither River Sediment Research. Keynote Address. Proc. 4th Int. Symposium on River Sedimentation. Post Symposium Volume, Beijing (China), 1989.
158. Kennedy, R.G. The Prevention of Silting in Irrigation Canals. Paper No. 2826, Proc. Inst. of Civil Engineers (London), Vol. 119, 1895.
159. Keulegan, G.H. Laws of Turbulent Flow in Open Channels. U. S Department of Commerce, NBS, Vol. 21, Dec. 1938.
160. Kerssens, P.J.M. and L.C. Van Rijn. Model for Unsteady Suspended Sediment Transport. Publ. No. 191, Delft Hydraulics Laboratory, Nov. 1977.
161. Khosla, A. N. Silting of Reservoirs. C.B.I.P. Publ.No. 51, New Delhi, 1953.
162. Kikkawa, H., S. Ikeda and A. Kitagawa. Flow and Bed Topography in Curved Open Channels. JHD, Proc. ASCE, Vol. 102. No. Hy-9, Sept. 1976.
163. Knighton, A. D. Short Term Changes in Hydraulic Geometry. In "River Channel Processes (Ed) K J Gregory. Wiley Inter Science, 1977.
164. Koelzer, V.A. and J. M. Lara. Densities and Compaction Rates of Deposited Sediment. JHD, Proc. ASCE, Vol. 84, No. 2, April, 1958.
165. Kondap, D.M. Some Aspects of Flow in Stable Alluvial Channels. Ph.D Thesis, University of Roorkee, Roorkee, 1977.
166. Kondratev, N. E. River Flow and River Channel Formation. Israel Programme of Scientific Translations, Jerusalem, 1962.
167. Krey, H. Grenzen der Ubertragbarkeit der Versuchserge — bnisse. Z. angew. Math. Mech. Bd.5, Heft 6, 1925.
168. Krumbein, W.C. A History of Principles and Methods of Mechanical Analysis. Jour. of Sed. Petrology. Vol. 2, No. 2, August 1932.
169. Lacey, G. Stable Channels in Alluvium. Min. Proc. of Inst. of Civil Engineers, (London), Vol. 229, 1929.
170. Lacey, G. and W. Pemberton. A General Formula for Uniform Flow in Self-formed Alluvial Channels. Proc. Inst. of Civil Engineers (London), Vol. 53, Pt.2, Tech. Note 71, 1972.
171. Lal, R.(Ed). Soil Erosion Research Methods. Soil and Water Conservation Society, Ankeny, Iowa (USA), 1988.
172. Lane, E. W. Stable Channels in Erodible Material. Trans. ASCE, Vol. 102, 1937.
173. Lane, E.W. and A.A. Kalinske. The Relation of Suspended Load to Bed Material in Rivers. Trans. A G U. Vol. 20, 1939.
174. Lane, E.W. and A. A. Kalinske. Engineering Calculations of Suspended Sediment. Trans. A G U, Vol. 22, 1941.
175. Lane, E. W. History of the Science of Sediment Transportation and Deposition (Unpublished Notes), 1955.
176. Lane, E. W. Importance of Fluvial Morphology in Hydraulic Engineering. Proc. ASCE, Paper 745, July, 1955.
177. Lane, E.W., P.N. Lin and H. K. Liu. The Most Efficient Stable Channel for Comparatively Clear Water in Non-cohesive Materials. Report of Civil Engg. Dept., Colorado State University, Fort Collins (USA), 1959.
178. Langbein, W. B. Hydraulic Criteria for Sand Waves. Trans. AGU, 1942.
179. Langbein, W. B. Geometry of River Channels. JHD, Proc. ASCE, Vol. 90, Hy-2, March, 1964.
180. Laursen, E.M. Total Sediment Load of Streams. JHD, Proc. ASCE, Vol. 84, No. Hy-1, Feb. 1958.
181. Lavelle, J.W. and W.C. Thacker. Effect of Hindered Settling on Sediment Concentration Profiles. JHR, IAHR, Vol. 16, No. 4, 1974.
182. Lechalas, C. Les Rivieres a Fond de Sable. Annales des Ponts et Chausseés, No. 1, 1871.
183. Lee, H.Y. and A.J. Odgaard. Simulation of Bed Armouring in Alluvial Channels. JHE, Proc. ASCE, Vol. 112, No. 9, Sept. 1986.
184. Leliavsky, S. An Introduction to Fluvial Hydraulics. Constable and Co. Ltd., London, 1954.
185. Leopold, L.B. and T. Maddock. The Hydraulic Geometry of Stream Channels and Some Physiographic Implications. USGS Prof. Paper 252, 1953.

186. Leopold, L.B. and M.G. Wolman. River Meanders. Bull. Geo. So. of Am., Vol. 71, 1960.

187. Lindley, E.S. Regime Channels. Proc. Punjab Engg. Congress. Vol. 7, 1919.

188. Little, W.C. and P.G. Meyer. The Role of Sediment Gradation on Channel Armouring. School of Civil Engineering, Georgia Institute of Technology, USA, ERC-0672, 1972.

189. Liu, H.K. and S.Y. Hwang. Discharge Formula for Straight Alluvial Channels. Trans. ASCE, Vol. 126, 1961.

190. Lobeck, A. L. Geomorphology. McGraw Hill Book Co U.S.A 1939.

191. Long, Yuqian. Manual on Operational Methods for the Measurement of Sediment Transport. Operational Hydrology Report No. 29, WMO-No. 686, 1989.

192. Mackin, J.G. Concept of Graded River. Bull. of Geo. So of Am., Vol. 59, 1948.

193. Mahmood, K. and R.N. Tarar. Field Research in Large Sand Bed Channels. Rivers, 76, Vol. II, ASCE, 1976.

194. Manthem, A.A. and D.V. De Munter — Thompson. Grove Karl Gilbert (1843-1918). Atlas, Vol. 4, No. 4, Dec.1968.

195. Matthes, G. H. Basic Aspects of Stream Meanders. Trans. AGU, Pt. 3, Vol. 22, 1941.

196. Mavis, F.T., C. Ho and V.C. Tu. The Transportation of Detritus by Flowing Water — I. Studies in Engg., University of Iowa, Bulletin 5, New Series No. 294, Iowa City, USA, March, 1935.

197. Mavis, F.T., T. Y. Liu and E. Soucek. The Transportation of Detritus by Flowing Water — II. Studies in Engineering, University of Iowa, Bulletin 11, New Series No. 34, Iowa University, USA, 1937.

198. McTigue, D. F. Mixture Theory of Suspended Sediment Transport. JHD, Proc. ASCE, Vol. 107, No. HY-6, June, 1981.

199. Mei, C.C. Non-uniform Diffusion of Suspended Sediment. JHD, Proc. ASCE, Vol. 95, No. HY-1, Jan. 1969.

200. Mehta, P.J., R. J. Garde and K. G. Ranga Raju. Transient Bed Profiles in Aggrading Streams. Proc. 2nd Int. Conference on River Sedimentation, Nanjing (China), 1983.

201. Mehta, A. J. *et al.* Cohesive Sediment Transport – I: Process Description. JHE, Proc. ASCE, Vol. 115, No. Hy-8, August, 1989.

202. Mehta, A. J. *et al.* Cohesive Sediment Transport – II: Application JHE, Proc. ASCE, Vol. 115, No. Hy-8 Aug. 1989.

203. Meyer-Peter, E. and R. Müller. Formulas for Bed-Load Transport. Proc. of 2nd Congress of IAHR, Stockholm, 1948.

204. Misri, R.L. and K. G. Ranga Raju. Bed-Load Transport of Non-uniform Sediment. Symposium on River Engineering and its Interaction with Hydrological and Hydraulic Research, Belgrade (Yugoslavia), 1980.

205. Mital, K.V. History of Thomason College of Engineering (1847-1947). University of Roorkee, Roorkee (UP), 1986.

206. Navntoft, E. A Theory of the Velocity and Suspended Load Distribution in Two-Dimensional Steady Uniform Open Channel Flow. Report No. 3, Danish Centre for Applied Mathematics and Mechanics, Tech. Univ. of Denmark, July 1970.

207. N. de Leliavsky. Currents in Streams and the Formation of Stream Beds. 6th Congress on International Navigation, Hague, 1894.

208. Newton, C. T. Experimental Investigation of Bed Degradation in an Open Channel. Trans. Boston Society of Civil Engineers, 1951.

209. Ning Chien. Meyer Peter Formula for Bed-Load Transport and Einstein Bed-Load Function. IER, MRD Series, No. 7, 1954.

210. Ning Chien. A Concept of Regime Theory. Trans. ASCE. Vol. 122, 1957.

211. Ning Chien *et al.* Mechanics of Sediment Transport. Science Publishing House, China, 1983.

212. Ning Chien *et al.* Fluvial Processes. Science Publishing House, China, 1987.

213. Nomicos, G.N. Effects of Sediment Load on the Velocity Field and Friction Factor on Turbulent Flow in an Open Channel. Ph.D Thesis, California Institute of Technology, Pasadena (USA), 1958.

214. Nordin, C.F. Statistical Properties of Dune Profiles. Ph.D Thesis, Colorado State University, Fort Collins (USA), 1968.

215. Obrien, M. P. Review of the Theory of Turbulent Flow and its Relation to Sediment Transportation. Trans. AGU, Vol 14, 1933.

216. Odgaard, A.J. and J.F. Kennedy. River Bed Bank Protecton by Submerged Vanes. JHE, Proc. ASCE, Vol. 109, No. HY-8, Aug. 1983.

217. Palaniappan, A.B. Numerical Modelling of Aggradation and Degradation in Alluvial Streams. Ph.D. Thesis, University of Roorkee, Roorkee, April 1991.

218. Pang, Y.H. Abhangigkeit der Geschiebewegung Von der Kornform und der Temperatur. Mitt. Pruss. Versuchsanst, Wasser, Erds, Schifftsbau, Berlin, Heft 37.

219. Parker, G. Sediment Inertia as a Cause of Antidunes. JHD, Proc. ASCE, Vol. 101, No. HY-2, Feb.1975.

220. Parker, G. On the Cause and Characteristics Scales of Meandering and Braiding in Rivers. JFM, Vol. 76, Pt.3, 1976.

221. Parker, G. Self Formed Straight Rivers with Equilibrium Bank and Mobile Bed, Pt. 2 : The Gravel River. JFM, VoJ. 89, P. Hy-1, 1978.

222. Parker, G. and E. D. Andrews. Sorting of Bed-Load Sediment by Flow in Meandering Bends. W. R. Research, Vol. 21, No. 9, 1985.

223. Parker P. A. M. Control of Rivers. George Routledge and Sons Ltd. 1925.

224. Partiot. H. L. Memoire Sur les Sables de la Loire. Annales des Ponts et Chausseés, No. 1. 1871.

225. Parsheniades. E. Erosion and Deposition of Cohesive Soils. JHD. Proc. ASCE. Vol 91, No. Hy-1. Jan. 1965.

226. Pazis, G.C. and W. H. Graf. Weak Sediment Transport, JHD, Proc. ASCE, Vol. 103, No. HY-7, July 1977.

227. Prandtl, L. and O. G. Tietjens. Fundamentals of Hydro and Aeromechanics; and Applied Hydo- and Aeromechanics. Dover Publications Inc. New York, 1934.

228. Proffitt, G. T. and A.J. Sutherland. Transport of Non-uniform Sediments. JHR, IAHR, Vol. 21, No. 1, 1983.

229. Qadar, A. The Vortex Scour Mechanism at Bridge Piers Ph.D. Thesis, Aligarh Muslim University, Aligarh, 1980.

230. Quraishy, M. S. River Meandering and the Earth's Rotation. Current Science, Oct. 1943.

231. Rahuel, J.L., F.M. Holly Jr., J. P. Chollet., P.J. Belleudy and G. Yang. Modelling of River Bed Evolution for Bed-Load Sediment Mixtures. JHE, Proc. ASCE, Vol. 115, No. Hy-11, 1989.

232. Ramete, M. A. Theoretical Approach on Fluvial Processes. Paper C-16, Int. Symposium on River Sedimentation, China, May 1980.

233. Raudkivi, A. J. On the Transport of Bed- Load by Waves. JHR, IAHR, Vol. 27, No. 2, 1989.

234. Rottner, J.A. Formula for Bed-Load Transportation. La Houille Blanche, No. 3, 1959.

235. Rozovskii, I. L. Flow of Water in Bends of Open Channels. Academy of Sciences of Ukranian SSR. Kiev, 1957.

236. Rouse, H. Fluid Mechanics for Hydraulic Engineers. McGraw Hill Book Co., New York, 1938.

237. Rouse, H. Experiments on the Mechanics of Sediment Suspension. Proc. of 5th Int. Congress on Applied Mechanics, Cambridge (Mass), USA, 1938.

238. Rouse, H. Modern Conceptions of the Mechanics of Fluid Turbulence. Trans. ASCE, Vol. 102, 1937.

239. Rouse, H. and S. Ince. History of Hydraulics. Iowa Institute of Hydraulic Research, State University of Iowa, USA, 1957.

240. Rubey, W. W. Settling Velocity of Gravels, Sands and Silt Particles. Am Jour. Sc., Vol. 25, No. 148, 1933.

241. Rubey, W. W. Equilibrium Conditions in Debris Laden Streams. Trans. AGU, 1933.

242. Rubey, W.W. The Force Required to Move Particles on a Stream Bed. USGS Prof. Paper 189-E, 1938.

243. Samaga, B. R. Total Load Transport of Sediment Mixtures. Ph.D. Thesis, University of Roorkee, Roorkee, 1984.

244. Sato, S., H. Kikkawa and K. Ashida. Research on Bed-Load Transportation. Public Works Research Institute, Japan, Vol. 28, 1958.

245. Sayre, W. W. and D. W. Hubbell. Transport and Dispersion of Labelled Bed Material — North Loup River, Nebraska. USGS Professional Paper 433-C, 1965.

246. Schoklitsch, A. Hydraulic Structures. ASME, 1937.

247. Schroeder, K. B. and C.H. Hembree. Application of Modified Einstein Procedure for Computation of Total Sediment Load. Trans. AGU, Vol. 37, 1956.

248. Shen, H. W. and C. S. Hung. An Engineering Approach to Total Bed Material Load by Regression Analysis. Proc. of the Sedimentation Symposium to Honour, Prof. Einstein. U.S.A. Chapter 14, 1972.

249. Shen, H. W. Hans Albert Einstein's Contribution in Sedimentation. JHD, Proc. ASCE, Vol. 101, No. Hy-5, May 1975.

250. Shen, H. W. Considerations of the Construction of Stochastic Sediment Bed-Load Models for Flat Bed. 3 rd Int. Symp. on Stochastic Hydraulics, Japan,1980.

251. Shen, H. W. and T. Y. Liu. Development and Prediction of Bed Armouring. JHD, Proc. ASCE, Vol. 109, No. Hy-4, Aprl.1983.

252. Shields, A. Awendung der Achnlickheitsmechanik und der Turbulenzforschung auf die Geschiebebewegung. Mitteilungen der Pruessischen Versuchsanstalt fur Wasserbau und Schiffbau, Berlin, 1936.

253. Simons, D. B. and M. L. Albertson. Uniform Water Conveyance Channels in Alluvial Material, Trans. ASCE, Vol. 128, Pt. I, 1963.

254. Smerdon, E. J. and R.P. Beasley. Critical Tractive Forces in Cohesive Soils. Agricultural Engineering, USA, Jan. 1961.

255. Sonderegger, A. L. The Effect of Regulation of Rio Grande on Flood Conditions below Elephant Butte Dam. Trans. ASCE, Vol. 100, 1935.

256. Song, C.S. and C. T. Yang. Velocity Profile and Minimum Stream Power. JHD, Proc. ASCE, Vol. 105, No. Hy-8, Aug.1979.

257. Soni, J.P., R. J. Garde and K. G. Ranga Raju. Aggradation in Streams Due to Overloading. JHD, Proc. ASCE, Vol. 106, No. Hy-1, Jan 1980.

258. Spring, F.J.E. River Training and Control: On the Guide Bank System. Tech. Paper No. 153, Govt. of India Press, 1903.

259. Sternberg, H. Untersuchungen Uber des Longen und Querprofil Gescheihefuhrender Flusse. Z Bauwesen, Vol. 25, 1875.

260. Sugio, S. A Study of the Sedimentation Upstream of a Weir in a Rectangular Flume by Means of Dimensional Analysis. Trans. JSCE, No. 80, 1962.

261. Suszka, L. and W. L. Graf. Sediment Transport in Steep Channels at Unsteady Flows. Proc. 22nd Congress of IAHR, Laussane (Switzerland), Vol. 1, 1987.

262. Swamee, P. K. and R. J. Garde. Progressive Reduction of Reservoir Capacity due to Sedimentation. Research Rep. of the Hyd. Engg. Section of Dept. of Civil Engg. Univ. of Roorkee, Roorkee, 1977.

263. Tanaka, S. and S. Sugimoto. On the Distribution of Suspended Sediment in Experimental Flume Flow. Memoirs of the Faculty of Engineering, Kobe University, Japan, No. 5, 1958.

264. Thomas, R. A. and. A. Paton. Claude Cavendish Inglis. Diamond Jubilee Souvenir 1916-1976, Central Water and Power Research Station, Pune, 1976.

265. Thompson, J. On the Origin and Winding of Rivers in Alluvial Plains with Remarks on Flow Around Bends in Pipes. Proc. RSL, Mar. 1876.

266. Thompson, J. R. A Study of the Variation of the Friction Factor in Alluvial Channels. M. S. Thesis, Dept. of Civil Engg. California State University, Long Beach, USA, 1988.

267. Thorne, C. R. Obituary of Brig. R A Bagnold. IAHR Bulletin, Vol. 7, No. 5, 1990.

268. Tiffnay, T.B. Studies of Meandering of Model Streams. Trans. AGU, Vol. 20, Aug. 1939.

269. Tinney, E. R. The Process of Channel Degradation in Alluvial Channels. JGR, Vol. 67, No. 4, April 1962.

270. Toffaleti, F. B. Definitive Computations of Sand Discharge in Rivers. JHD, Proc. ASCE, Vol. 95, No. Hy-1, Jan 1969.

271. Tsujimoto, T. Effects of Unsteadiness, Non-uniformity and Relaxation on Bed-Load Transport. Proc. Int. Conference on Fluvial Hydraulics, Budapest (Hungary), 1986.

272. USDA. Proceedings of the Rainfall Simulator Workshop. Tucson, Arizona (USA), ARM-W-10, Montana, 1979.

273. USDA. CREAMS — A Field Scale Model for Chemicals, Runoff, and Erosion for Agricultural Management Systems. Conservation Research Rep. 26, Science and Education Administration, Washington, DC, 1980.

274. US Govt. and IIHR. A Study of Measurement and Analysis of Sediment Loads in Streams. Development and Calibration of V. A. Tube; Report No. 11, 1957.

275. USWES. Sediment Investigations on the Mississippi River and its Tributaries Prior to 1930. Paper H, 1936.

276. Vanoni, V.A. Transportation of Suspended Sediment by Running Water. Trans. ASCE, Vol. 111, 1946.

277. Vanoni, V. A. Fifty Years of Sedimentaton. JHE, Proc. ASCE, Vol. 10, No. 8, Aug. 1984.

278. Varshney, D. V. Scour Around Bends in Alluvial Channels. Ph.D Thesis, University of Roorkee, Roorkee, 1973.

279. Vaze, K.V. Pracheen Hindu Shilpa Shastra (In Marathi) published by Vaze, Nasik, 1924, Chapter VI.

280. Vaze, K. V. Importance of Engineering Education (in Marathi).

281. Vetter, C.F. Why desilting Works for All American Canals. Engineering New Record, Vol. 118, No. 8, 1937.

282. Vetter, C. P. Sediment Problems in Lake Mead and Downstream of the Colorado River. Trans. AGU, Vol. 30, Apr. 1953.

283. Vetter, M. Gesamttransport Von Sedimenten in Offenon Gerinnen. Mitt. des Institut fur Wasserwesen. Univ. der Bundeswehr, Munich, Heft 26/1988.

284. Vittal, N., K.G. Ranga Raju, and R. J. Garde. Sediment Transport Relations Using Concept of Effective Shear Stress. Proc. Int. Symposium on River Mechanics, IAHR, Bangkok (Thailand), 1973.

285. Voinieh — Syanozhenstki, T. G. and N. E. Kereselidze. Generation of Morphological Macrostructures by Non Stationarity of Bed Streams and Their Evolution. Proc. 16th Congress of IAHR, Istambul, Vol. 2, 1975.

286. Werner, P.W. On the Origin of River Meanders. Trans. AGU, Vol. 32, No. 6, Dec. 1951.

287. White, C.M. The Equilibrium of Grains on the Bed of Stream. Proc. RSL. Series - A. Mathematical and Physical Sciences. Vol. 174, No. 958, Feb. 1940.

288. White, W.R., E. Paris, and R. Bettess. River Regime Based on Sediment Transport. Rep. No. JJ, 201, Hyd. Res. Station, Wallingford (UK), 1981.

289. Wischmeier, W.H. and D.D. Smith. Predicting Rainfall Erosion Losses. Agriculture Handbook, No. 537, USDA, Washington, D C, 1978.

290. Xu Muju. Sediment Problems at Dujiangyan Project. Jour. of Sediment Research, China, Vol. 3, No. 1, 1981.

291. Yadav, H.S. Bed Level Variation in Alluvial Streams, Ph. D. Thesis, University of Roorkee, Roorkee, 1992.

292. Yalin, M.S. An Expression for Bed-Load Transportation. JHD, Proc. ASCE, Vol. 89, No. Hy-3, May 1963.

293. Yalin, M.S. Mechanics of Sediment Transport. Pergamon Press, Ltd. Oxford, U. K. 1972.

294. Yalin, M.S. and E. Karahan. Steepness of Sedimentary Dunes. JHD, Proc. ASCE, Vol. 105, No. HY-4, Apr. 1979.

295. Yalin, M.S. and E. Karahan. Inception of Sediment Transport. JHD, Proc. ASCE, Vol. 105, No. HY-11, Nov. 1979.

296. Yang, C.T. Incipient Motion and Sediment Transport. JHD, Proc. ASCE, Vol. 99, No. Hy-10, Oct. 1973.

297. Yang, C. T. Minimum Unit Stream Power and Fluvial Hydraulics. JHD, Proc. ASCE, Vol. 102, No. Hy-7, July 1974.

298. Yellow River Conservancy Commission. Selected Papers of Researches on the Yellow River and Present Practice. Oct. 1987.

299. Yucel, O. and Graf W.H. Bed Load Deposition in Reservoirs. Proc. of 15th Congress of IAHR, Istambul, Vol. 1, 1973.

300. Zhang Hou and R. Kahawita. Non-Linear Model for Aggradation in Alluvial Channels. JHE, Proc. ASCE, Vol. 113, No. Hy-3, Mar. 1987.

301. Zhang, Q., J.Yue, Z. Duan and M. Dai. A Mathematical Model For Prediction of Sedimentation Process in River. Proc. 2nd Int. Symposium on River Sedimentation. IRTCES, Nanging (China), 1983.

302. Zimmerman, C. and J.F. Kennedy. Transverse Bed Slopes in Curved Alluvial Streams. JHD, Proc. ASCE, Vol. 104, No. Hy-1, Jan 1978.

303. Zwamborn, J.A. Reproducibility in Hydraulic Models of Prototype River Morphology. La Houille Blanche. No. 3, 1966.

304. Zwamborn, J.A. Solution of River Problems with Movable Bed Hydraulic Models. Nat. Mech. Engg. Res. Institute, CSIR, MEG 597, South Africa, 1967.

Author Index

Subject Index